GOSPEL CHOIRS

GOSPEL CHOIRS

Psalms of Survival
for an Alien Land Called Home

Best Wishes,

Derrick Bell

D ERRICK B ELL

BasicBooks
A Division of HarperCollins*Publishers*

Grateful acknowledgment is made for permission to reprint from the following:
"Look How Far We've Come" written by Milton Biggham. Copyright © 1991 by Arisav Music. All rights reserved. Used by permission.
"I Don't Feel No Ways Tired" by Curtis Burrell. Copyright © 1977 by Savgos Music. All rights reserved. Used by permission.
Rev. F. C. Barnes, "Rough Side of the Mountain." Copyright © 1983 by Eternal Gold Music.
"I Just Want to Make It to the Other Side" by the Rev. F. C. Barnes. Used by permission of Atlanta International Music Company.
"Speak to My Heart" written by Donnie McClurkin. Copyright © 1990 by Savros Music/Don-Mac Music. All rights reserved. Used by permission.
"Trouble Don't Last Always" written by Timothy Wright. Copyright © 1991 by Arisav Music. All rights reserved. Used by permission.
"The Battle Is The Lord's" by V. Michael McKay. Used with the permission of V. Michael McKay and Schaff Publishing, copyright © 1993.
"We've Come This Far by Faith" by Albert A. Goodson. Copyright © 1963, renewed 1991 by Manna Music, Inc., 35255 Brooten Road, Pacific City, Oregon 97135. All rights reserved. Used by permission.
From *Saint Peter Relates an Incident* by James Weldon Johnson. Copyright © 1917, 1921, 1935 by James Weldon Johnson, copyright renewed © 1963 by Grace Nail Johnson. Used by permission of Viking Penguin, a division of Penguin Books USA, Inc.
From *Collected Poems* by Langston Hughes. Copyright © 1994 by the Estate of Langston Hughes. Reprinted by permission of Alfred A. Knopf, Inc.

FIRST EDITION

Library of Congress Cataloging-in-Publication Data

Bell, Derrick A.
    Gospel choirs : psalms of survival for an alien land called home /
Derrick Bell.
        p.   cm.
    Includes bibliographical references and index.
    ISBN 0–465–02412–2
    1. Afro-Americans—Fiction. 2. Christian fiction, American. 3. Allegories.
I. Title.
PS3552.E497G67   1996
813' .54—dc20   96-6250

96 97 98 99 00 ❖/HC 10 9 8 7 6 5 4 3 2 1

To Ada Elizabeth Bell, my mother;
to Janet Dewart Bell, my wife—
out of my belief in the potential of women to save us all.

O black and unknown bards of long ago,
How came your lips to touch the sacred fire?

Heart of what slave poured out such melody
As "Steal away to Jesus"? On its strains
His spirit must have nightly floated free,
Though still about his hands he felt his chains.
Who heard great "Jordan Roll"? Whose starward eye
Saw chariot "swing low"? And who was he
That breathed that comforting melodic sigh,
"Nobody knows de trouble I see"?

— James Weldon Johnson

CONTENTS

~

PROLOGUE

We're not here for no form or fashion,
but to sing the praises of the Lord. *

For gospel singers, the Biblical suggestion *"make a joyful noise*
unto the Lord" is less admonition than invitation to renew,
through song, the faith of our forebears. Gladly, and without
pretense or frivolity, these singers praise the Lord through the
intricacies of lyric, melody, rhythm, harmony. Rooted deep in
black culture, blessed with talent, honed in belief, they and
their music comfort the afflicted, console the bereaved,
strengthen the weak, reassure the discouraged, and bring to all
within the sound of their voices a soulful joy.

Long ago, the slave singers, by interweaving melody and
lyric in songs of faith—the spirituals—were able to transcend
the awful oppression that defined their lives. Embracing religion that was undergirded by this music helped slaves to be
free in their own minds. It gave their imaginations nourishment
for creating a world of freedom where they could be whoever
they felt they truly were—not just someone's chattel who was
worked, beaten, raped, maimed, sold, and killed for profit or

*The sources for all epigraphs, quotations, statistics, and specific factual informa-
tion will be found in the notes, keyed by page, beginning on page 217.

sport. The music, encompassing all of this despair, empowers the singers with a faith and determination that thrills the heart and nurtures the soul.

At a later time, and especially after black people began immigrating to the North, those we now call gospel singers updated the music of black religion—many of the spirituals, of course, but also standard hymns and newly written songs. Church-connected composers revised the slave singers' messages about the trials of this life which would be rewarded by life after death. To this basic and still prevalent theme, they added an optimistic outlook about the present. The "good news," the "gospel truth," was, they suggested, that, through faith and adherence to Jesus's teachings, happiness could be achieved in this life.

Emancipation, while it ended slavery, did not bring freedom. The lives of black people were filled with trouble and hard times. Their daily experiences suggested that the future, as far as they could see or imagine, offered only more anguish, more woes. And yet, using the idiom and instruments of jazz and the blues, gospel composers wrote, and their choirs sang with assurance, "I'm So Glad, Trouble Don't Last Always." Lifting their voices in complex harmonies, marvelous cadences, and with rhythms beyond anything despair could silence, they imbued meaning beyond the words to the pledge "I'm Going to Live the Life I Sing About in My Song."

Bernice Johnson Reagon, founder and lead singer of the singing group Sweet Honey and the Rock, explains the magical pull of this music. In singing in a black style, "you have to be able to change the notes with feelings before the sound comes out of your body. . . . So you are not singing notes and tones, you are giving out pieces of yourself, coming from places inside that you can only yourself visit in a singing. It is having what is inside yourself ride the air in the song you are singing." The result, as the sociologist Paul Gilroy might put it, is music that serves as "an enhanced mode of communication beyond the petty power of words—spoken or written." But it is as well a do-it-yourself vehicle to personal salvation, able to encompass life's troubles and disappointments.

In this music dwells the stuff of miracles. For black people it has been and remains, as the novelist Alice Walker believes, "inoculation against poison, immunization against the disease of racist and sexist selfishness, envy, and greed." And in its ability to express "all the connectedness that racist oppression and colonial destruction tried to keep hidden," black music communicates a political as well as a religious dimension. During the slave era, it helped bind the disparate peoples of Africa into a single community. While praising Jesus, the words of those songs also contained directions for those black men and women planning to escape slavery and head for freedom in the North. A century later, during the civil rights movement, black and white protesters, who risked well-being and their lives to abolish Jim Crow laws, found strength in songs written by slaves and transformed them into "Freedom Songs." And today it is no accident that black students, including those enrolled in the nation's most prestigious colleges, form gospel choirs. Even these most fortunate descendants of the enslaved recognize and reach out for the spiritual nourishment that is the essence of this music's appeal.

Gospel, and particularly the gospel choir at its best, echoes the tempos of the soul searching for God's peace in the midst of a hostile world. Gospel music buoys our spirits as we learn during what Susan Taylor calls "the journal of a lifetime," during which we discover the "aspect of our being that is invulnerable and immortal." There is in gospel music a universality capable of touching all who hear and need its comfort, its consolation. Who among us, of whatever race, color, class, or creed, can hear gospel music without surrendering to the felt need to tap a foot, sway just a bit, perhaps even join in when the hand clapping really gets going? Truly, this music speaks to the unavoidable fact that, at bottom, we are all in the same boat.

There is potential in this music to touch and unite across barriers of race and class. Who knows? Gospel music has already "crossed over" and is popular in portions of the white community. Perhaps gospel music is the much-sought link that can unite the people of this nation across barriers of race and color, class and creed, enabling all of our souls to "ride the air in the songs [we] are singing."

∽

> *Look how far we've come with the Lord,*
> *Look how far we've come with the Lord,*

Musing about the power and potential of gospel music, I found myself swaying to the recorded rhythms of the gospel song joyously sung by the Dallas/Fort Worth Mass Choir.

> *We've come through hard trials, tribulations,*
> > *persecutions,*
> *Here we stand,*
> *Look how far we've come with the Lord.*

I wondered, as the rich choral sound filled my home office. Could the ultimate optimism of this gospel hymn—and others like it—provide black people with the insight to comprehend, the courage to confront, the wisdom to find new solutions to our greatest crisis since the end of Reconstruction? A sea of papers, studies, statistics, all documenting that crisis, surrounded me and my computer. My immediate challenge was to transform this evidence of our increasingly dire plight into a written warning, one sufficiently clear to challenge us to action, but not so devastating as to encourage denial or suggest surrender. A warning that would serve to confirm what many of us know but are afraid to acknowledge, that the present suffering of so many could foretell the future fate of us all.

It is easy to dismiss my concerns as the worn rhetoric of a disillusioned veteran of too many civil rights battles lost when I thought them won. But experience can bring wisdom as well as disillusionment. I can see more clearly than I have been able to articulate the triple threat blacks face today.

First. The status of most blacks is steadily getting worse. The numbers tell the story. Black unemployment is more than twice the overall rate; black income is only 60 percent that of whites; long-term joblessness has devastated individuals, their families, their communities; the prisons are filled with black men who have turned to crime. I have all the data, but of what value are statistics? So many blacks feel overwhelmed by their evidence of devastation, and so many whites view them as sufficient proof of black sloth, black unreadiness.

Racial rationalizations should not be a surprise. They serve now, as throughout the nation's history, as a convenient and comforting substitute for the economic well-being and social status most whites lack. A working-class white man, with a lack of empathy that is surely widespread, dismissed 1995's Million Man March as an empty publicity stunt. As soon as the men return home, he predicted, "they're going to be back on food stamps, back on welfare. Blacks are always talking about discrimination—the white man is doing this, the white man is doing that. It's everybody's fault but theirs. I don't think that's going to change." Another white said that if a black, a Hispanic, and a white apply for a job, "it's pretty much always going to be the black man gets the job because he's black."

Employers, aware of the susceptibility of many whites to accept racial explanations for job rejections, are quite willing to blame affirmative action whenever they are unwilling to hire or promote a white person. Indeed, if employers were required to pay a modest tax each time they lie and tell a rejected white job applicant that he or she cannot be hired because the company is required to hire a black, the national debt would be reduced substantially. It is far harder to explain why some whites so gullibly accept race-blaming rationales than it is to predict why few will believe Labor Secretary Robert Reich's report that black men have been hit hardest by structural changes in the economy. He reports that only 50 percent of black men were able to maintain full-time, full-year employment in the 1980s, compared with 75 percent in the 1970s. "If you compare white men, white women, black men and black women," Reich concludes, "black men have fallen farthest and hardest in terms of wages, benefits and employment."

Excluded from the mainstream of American life, an increasing number of black individuals and families are crippled by poverty and all the unhappy consequences of life without money in a society where well-being, status, and self-regard are all measured in monetary terms. The predictable results: drug-related crime that has filled the nation's prisons with record numbers of black men, disorganized families, derelict schools, teenage parents, lifeless communities.

Second. The economic distress blacks are suffering is a dramatic illustration of the technological revolution that is eliminating work as the cornerstone of the nation's stability. But in recent years, growing reliance on automation, the deportation of jobs to third-world countries, and the importation of cheap foreign labor have all worsened the unemployment problem. Many of the nation's largest corporations are reducing their employment rolls by thousands of workers in order to maintain or even enhance profit levels. As a result, there are growing numbers of once-employed and now-unemployed skilled workers, both white collar and blue collar, executives and professionals. Advances in computer and communication technology have rendered much of their work superfluous, and the availability of cheap and exploitable foreign labor has proven a temptation few company heads seem able to resist. Even the largest companies now hire on a part-time basis or contract work out as needed.

These arrangements usually involve low pay, few benefits, and no security. In the meantime, corporate executives' earnings are soaring. Between 1977 and 1990, salaries of top executives in American corporations rose by 220 percent. Had the nation's manufacturing workers shared in the productivity gains and profits to the same extent as management, the average factory laborer today would be earning more than $81,000 per year. For these excessively salaried men (as most of them are), the God of the Prophets has become the god of profit.

As a result of short-term bottom-line policies, the great majority of American workers have experienced not only unprecedented job upheavals but also an absolute twenty-year decline in personal earnings. Unwilling to acknowledge the seriousness of the problem, government policy analysts continue to cite outmoded unemployment data—data that do not consider those no longer seeking work or those working in part-time, low-paid jobs. Even the far from progressive magazine *Business Week* ran a cover story titled "The Real Truth About the Economy: How Government Statistics Are Misleading Us." It warns that "Americans are right to be worried about jobs these days, despite the official unemployment rate." The article provides pages of data and charts to report about joblessness what so many now seeking work are experiencing firsthand. Policy analysts assure us that these economic ups and downs are to be expected. We need only to tough it out while waiting for the next upturn in the economy. The problem is that the economy is in good shape for the well-off. Everyone claims to deplore a recession; but, as John Kenneth Galbraith points out, a "great many people and an even higher proportion of those who have political voice and vote . . . find a recession quite comfortable, and certainly more so than the measures that do anything effective about it. This," he added, "no one dreams of saying."

The benefits of relatively high employment are no secret. They are available in the merger and downsizing stories reported in the business pages every day and in articles in progressive magazines and books. Corporations and, increasingly, government entities are announcing with pride—rather than appropriate shame—that they are laying off thousands of workers: *to cut costs*, they say; but *to enhance profits*, they mean. For even those companies reporting healthy profits are engaging in what amounts to a "downsizing" frenzy. These hard-hearted policies are making millions of dollars for a few people and have cost millions of Americans their jobs and placed millions more at risk.

And yet there was no discernible outcry when an international study on income distribution announced both that the income gap between the rich and the poor was wider in the United States during the 1980s than in any other large, industrialized country, and that the relatively high levels of inequality in this country persisted into the early 1990s. *The Economist* published more detail on income inequalities in America, finding them greater than at any time in the past fifty years. Ownership of wealth has always been extremely unequal in the United States. In 1929, the year of the stock-market crash that ushered in the Great Depression, the top 1 percent of households owned 36.3 percent of the nation's financial wealth. It has been suggested that, in ways hard to trace, this much wealth at the top serves as a giant "suction pump" siphoning the life out of the economy. By 1949, the share of financial wealth owned by the top 1 percent fell to a post-1929 low of 20.8 percent (one fifth), a result of New Deal legislation and wartime tax rates. After 1949, the trend toward less concentration reversed itself. Today, the top 1 percent of households own 37.0 percent (over one third) of the nation's financial wealth, a piece of the wealth pie slightly larger than their share in 1929. And the disparity continues to grow.

The media and all but a few government officials treat these disparities in income and wealth as phenomena without fault. They are just stated as natural occurrences, like an unusually hot summer, rather than attributed to the massive changes in business practices, including the government's deliberately allowing manufacturers to go overseas for cheap labor or importing ill-paid immigrants, thus losing millions of American jobs, while seriously undercutting such businesses as the textile, steel, and automobile industries.

Perhaps the unemployed do not rise up or pressure their elected representatives because they accept the stories predicting that technology will soon produce exciting new jobs. Edward Luttwack has sought to disabuse us of such wishful thinking. In the *Washington Post,* he warns that the exciting new high-tech companies will not hire many displaced workers—even those with ample skills and experience. He points, for example, to Intel, Microsoft, Apple Computer, and Genentech, which all together employ a grand total of 62,500 people—only 500 more than Home Depot alone, a retail chain that offers mostly low-paid and part-time jobs.

More likely, the vast majority of poor and working-class Americans no longer believe government is relevant to their lives. Most don't vote. All too many of those who do vote—swayed by appeals to their prejudices—vote against their interests. Sadly, Democrats and Republicans either ignore the economic plight of those without work or urge remedies that are irrelevant—more training for nonexistent jobs (the Democrats)—or counterproductive—lowering capital-gains taxes (the Republicans), a financial bonanza for the well-to-do who would chiefly benefit from such a reduction. Both parties—although in varying degrees—favor cutting entitlements for the poor, as though this further sacrifice of our neediest on the altar of free enterprise will allay the economic gods we worship despite the growing risks.

Third. History not only teaches but warns that, in periods of severe economic distress, the rights of blacks are eroded and the lives of blacks endangered. A century ago, when the U.S. economy was disrupted by the change from an agricultural to an industrial base, American blacks were already hated by large segments of society, particularly hard-pressed farmers in the South and factory workers—many of them recent immigrants—in the North. Black people were made a target for the wrath and frustration of the millions of white Americans being squeezed by that change in job patterns. Now the patterns of job loss and racial antagonism are worsening at the same time that perhaps a majority of whites believe that racial discrimination is hardly more than a convenient excuse for blacks who crave preferences while disdaining performance.

Callers and audience participants on a Phil Donahue show strongly indicated their view that anti-black feelings were a predictable reaction to affirmative action policies. Donahue, trying to ease the growing tension, said tongue-in-cheek, "Yes, I know. Are you telling me that every white person in America has a relative who lost out on a job or promotion to a less-qualified black?" To his obvious chagrin, the audience broke into wild applause. Clinging to a comforting myth, they missed Donahue's effort to use humor to illustrate a truth they are determined not to see.

The media, pandering to these racial myths, are unswervingly attracted to stories about black street crime or welfare cheats. Crime is a black problem. Relatively little attention is given to such white-collar crime as the savings-and-loan fiasco, for which all Americans are having to pay through their taxes. Mothers on welfare is another easy target, while the tremendous subsidies government provides corporate America seldom come under scrutiny.

African Americans are again condemned to suffer because of economic conditions we did not create. We not only are bearing the brunt of unemployment but are also the focus of the rage of the many whites who, fearful for their own jobs and future well-being, are all too easily convinced that the threat to both is our black presence rather than the real villain—corporate greed. And what of the future? At the least, we will need impressive wellsprings of faith to withstand a fate that could exacerbate the current hostility into major violence and bloodshed. It would not be the first time that black people were hunted down and massacred in the streets or cremated in their homes set ablaze by angry white mobs. Given this environment of black blame, the traditional sources of relief—the courts and the political process—are not likely to prove useful in the present crisis. They are, of course, still worthy of attention and effort, but they have proved themselves woefully inadequate to protect our lives, much less our rights.

"If not these remedies, then what?" I anticipated the question from civil rights advocates, and all evening had been wracking my brain in search of an answer. We need a foundation for new tactics that speaks directly to today's crisis, one that also encompasses the vehicles of faith and steadfastness that have served us so well in past struggles. A stack of gospel music recordings sparked my thinking and buoyed my spirits. There must be a connection between this music and how we utilized it in earlier ordeals and its potential for now. But how do I find the connection and—assuming I can—how convince others of my discovery?

Marvelous singing, but is the stuff there to overcome corporate power and the hypnotic spell it has cast over much of the populace? One would think not, but the power in this music does not spring from logic nor can it be calculated in statistical terms. And yet it helped overcome the most invidious system of slavery the world has ever seen.

Slavery has ended, but the assumptions of whites about their ascendance over blacks remains. I have long tried, with Geneva Crenshaw's help, to convey the basic truth about the ineradicableness of racism not as a scary premonition but as a challenge to think about the law and race in new ways, a challenge that would, whether won or lost, bring peace to the mind and solace to the soul. For a decade, Geneva and I have been collaborating on a series of stories she had envisioned during a years-long recovery from a near-fatal auto crash in Mississippi where, in the 1960s, we both handled civil rights litigation. While a fine lawyer, Geneva, as I came to know in the course of our friendship, also possesses strange powers and a prescience I can only call supernatural. One of a trio of godlike Sisters, the Celestial Curia, Geneva uses parables to illustrate her rare understanding of racial dynamics.

It was from her that I got the Chronicles on which I based my 1987 book *And We Are Not Saved: The Elusive Quest for Racial Justice*. In it, we demonstrated how society implemented its commitment to ending racial segregation—only to replace it with more effective, if less obvious, forms of white dominance. The new techniques, unlike the vanquished Jim Crow practices, were immune to legal attack.

In the five years between that and my second book, *Faces at the Bottom of the Well: The Permanence of Racism,* opportunities for even the most fortunate blacks diminished, while with the virtual closing of the job market, particularly in the inner cities, prospects for working-class blacks worsened dramatically. This situation is not an artifact of slavery, or evidence of intrinsic weakness in black people themselves, but integral to a social structure where the subordination of blacks serves many whites as a basis of personal identity and social stability. The "permanence" theme was not, as some thought, a signal of surrender, but a tardy recognition of racism's deepest roots.

"And some readers got our message," I murmured to myself.

"But not enough, my friend." A voice behind me jolted me out of my musings, almost out of my chair.

I looked behind me—and, sure enough, there she was.

Sitting on my couch, looking her usual regal self, even with her shoes off and her feet drawn up under her, was my lawyer friend and Curia Sister, Geneva Crenshaw. I was so pleased to see her that I didn't even think to grumble about her habit of simply appearing, rather than phoning ahead or even just ringing my bell like a normal person. I knew better than to complain anyway. "What's a little invasion of privacy among friends?" she would ask, and I'd have to agree.

For a moment I couldn't say anything. I just looked at her. Her beauty, arising as much from her interior as from her physical self, only deepens as she grows older. In describing her (as many readers ask me to do), I am drawn to the poetic, the lyrical. Glowing, magisterial, enigmatic, Geneva is the epitome of a sort of grace, an air I've noticed in other women who understand far more about the world than any mere man. The challenge for us men is to acknowledge (at least, to ourselves) this insight and not compete with or question it, certainly not resent it.

"So," I said, realizing she was reading my every thought, "am I getting sharper in assessing the value of women?"

"You are indeed!" she replied. "But," she added with a sly smile, "your learning curve has been painfully slow! And not only about women! I'm glad to see you're finally getting realistic about the serious dangers facing African Americans in this country. So far as I can see, it looks ever more like, as the Old Testament prophesies, 'God's Going to Rain Down Fire.'"

"I'm not going to blame God for the crisis I'm struggling with," I said, "when I have only to look at the self-destructive mode of our nation's leaders. You know, Geneva, I feel like Thomas Jefferson when long ago, while pondering the evils of slavery, he wrote, 'I tremble for my country when I reflect that God is just; that his justice cannot sleep forever.'"

Geneva nodded in somber agreement, then asked, "Didn't your last E-mail suggest you have some immediate and, I must add, self-imposed problems to deal with?"

I nodded. "I've agreed to appear tomorrow on one of what you call those 'mendacious' TV talk shows, specifically the conservative Biff Rightwing and his equally conservative audience, in the hope of showing them that they're hardly better off in terms of opportunity than the blacks they despise. And soon afterward, I'm meeting with a group of civil rights advocates who are furious at me about that article of mine suggesting how far the affirmative action backlash might go. That piece was, you may remember, based on one of your stories."

"Good luck, friend," Geneva replied, shaking her head, "but don't expect not to be frustrated when both groups are cemented in ideological rigidity. You and I could better be looking more closely at the division racism has wrought in black people themselves. That is, while I share your concern about what is being done to destroy us, I am equally troubled by what we are doing to destroy ourselves. We must persuade black people to review their relationships with one another, to refuse to accept this society's gender roles featuring male dominance and female subordination. While diluting and dissipating the inherent and developed strengths possessed by black women, such arrangements corrupt and diminish the inherent strengths of black men."

"You're surely right as to the result, Geneva, but aren't many black men being abusive and macho because they can't find the jobs that would enable them to provide for women and protect them?"

Geneva gave me a hard look. "Such abuse deserves excoriation, not defense!" she said. "All too often men, unable to find work, take their frustration out not on the people who deny them jobs, but on their own women. The pattern is as clear—and corrosive—as that whereby poor whites let their anger for their poor economic situation be deflected onto blacks, who are in fact as helpless as they are. Unless curbed and corrected by a new understanding of male-female relationships, such deflection of anger could crucially undermine our effort to survive.

"It is such an understanding I hope we can help develop

for your new book. We can only strengthen personal relationships if men reject male dominance and women reject subordinance. Both men and women must come to embrace mutual support as the critical prerequisite to rebuilding and reorganizing communities."

"But, Geneva," I protested, "even if blacks achieve a new togetherness through gender equality, nothing in the annals of this country justifies a prediction that our efforts will alter the destructive course of a nation where, as W. E. B. DuBois observed, the real allegiance is to reducing all the nation's resources to dusky dollars. In pursuit of that goal, native Americans were virtually wiped out, millions of Africans were enslaved, Asians and Mexicans were exploited, and millions of working-class whites have spent much of their lives in labor only a few steps less onerous than slavery."

"True enough, friend. But surrender is not an option, and struggle may enable some of us to survive and maintain our humanity. If we are never more than, as Harriet Tubman put it, 'strangers in a strange land,' with all that land's dangers, still we have managed to salvage much of our strength as a people from facing those dangers while singing the songs of Zion."

"That's it, Geneva! Either in the music itself, or in the determination to keep going, sparked and nurtured by the music, we must learn to do what our enslaved ancestors did. We do have resources. We—as Alice Walker observed, not in complaint but in celebration—'do not come from people who have had nothing. We come rather from people who've had everything—except money, except political power, except freedom.' Our challenge is to identify and harness our 'everything' to meet the current crisis.

"And, Geneva," I continued, "you may be right that a restructuring of gender relations will lead to a stronger black community, one better able to fend off the myriad manifestations of hostility we will most certainly face during the transformation and possible destruction of our economy. But do you think even your stories will be able to effect so major a change?'"

"I seem to remember your quite similar concern about our effort to get blacks to face up to the permanence of racism. And yet did not many of them do just that after reading 'The Space Traders' story in your last book?"

I nodded. "You're right, as usual. And that reminds me, Geneva. Many of our readers want to know what happens to all America's black people after they disappear into the Space Traders' airships."

"I have a story to start your new book that will answer their question. And not just your readers, friend." With a slight smile, Geneva reached in her bag and handed me several sheets of manuscript. "By the way, you are in it, too," she said.

"Me?"

She saw my look of surprised discomfort. "And myself as well," she added.

"But you!" I protested. "There's no reason for you to go. You have the power to return to the safety of your home with your Sisters Curia."

"Do you really think I would want to do that?" she asked gently. "That after all the struggles since the 1960s we have engaged in *together* "—and her emphasis was as of a sacred word—" I would not share that ordeal—whatever it might hold —with you and all my brothers and sisters down here? Is not sharing trouble with one's friends and family part of the implicit pledge we have each made to one another and to ourselves?"

At that moment, the voice of the great gospel singer Marion Williams flooded over us in one of Thomas A. Dorsey's familiar hymns.

"And that," Geneva said, after listening a moment, "is what I mean to do. 'I'm Going to Live the Life I Sing About in My Song.'"

1

⚛

REDEMPTION DEFERRED: BACK TO THE SPACE TRADERS

Soon-a will be done-a with the troubles of the world,
the troubles of the world, the troubles of the world.
Soon-a will be done-a with the troubles of the world,
Goin' home to live with God.

—Traditional Spiritual

History has convinced me that the rights and even lives of black people, even as citizens, have always been a commodity subject to barter by white people for their own needs and self-interest. This conviction became awful truth when aliens from some distant world swooped down on the United States, landed their gigantic ships along the outer beaches of Cape Cod, and made the nation an extraordinary offer: sufficient stores of gold to pay off its debts, chemicals to cleanse its environment, and a safe nuclear engine and fuel to replace disappearing fossil fuels. In return, these Space Traders wanted only one thing: to take away to their world all African Americans. The response: horror from virtually all blacks and some whites; barely restrained glee from many whites; much ambivalence from everyone else. After two weeks of furious debate, there was a national referendum on the issue: 70 percent of the citizenry voted yes, and the Trade went forward.

The last Martin Luther King holiday the nation would ever observe dawned on an extraordinary sight. In the night, the Space Traders had drawn their strange ships right up to the beaches and discharged their cargoes of gold, minerals, and machinery, leaving vast empty holds. Crowded on the beaches were the inductees, some twenty million silent black men, women, and children, including babes in arms. As the sun rose, the Space Traders directed them, first, to strip off all but a single undergarment; then, to line up; and finally, to enter those holds which yawned in the morning light like Milton's "darkness visible." The inductees looked fearfully behind them. But, on the dunes above the beaches, guns at the ready, stood U.S. guards. There was no escape, no alternative. Heads bowed, arms now linked by slender chains, black people left the new world as their forebears had arrived.

We passed through that curtain of darkness into a vast enclosure, a realm of light. Above us, around us, glowed and pulsated all the colors of the rainbow, dazzling my eyes, softening my grim expectations. From somewhere over our heads, a hidden voice spoke.

"Raise your arms and clap your hands."

This was no longer the clone of Ronald Reagan's voice, with which the Space Traders had opened and conducted their negotiations with the United States. This was definitely a black voice, warm and resonant. Whether a man's voice or a woman's, I couldn't tell.

As we raised our arms in response to the command, the

manacles and chains that bound our hands together and us to one another, fell off with a fearsome clattering.

"Look down!" Again, the voice, sounding now even more familiar, a harmonious blending of Ossie Davis and Ruby Dee. Obeying again, we found at our feet, not those emblems and instruments of our servitude, but a folded piece of beautifully woven cloth. We understood that we were to pick it up. As we did, each unfolded into a soft robe, which we put on to wrap around our near-nakedness.

"Take a deep breath," came the voice, "and stand perfectly still." The soft colors surrounding us coalesced into a brilliant flash of light. Behind me I heard Geneva's soft voice, "Keep the faith, friend!" Then, darkness.

I stood in place with everyone else, neither awake nor asleep, bound but immobilized, relaxed yet not lethargic, unable to act yet clear of mind. I knew that time was passing, but had no idea how much. I wondered, By what means—what miracle, really—have the Space Traders suspended our vital functions for the long journey back to their home star?

After unimaginable, immeasurable time, the light flashed again. And, again, the hidden voice spoke.

"Attention, African Americans! It is now two months, as you reckon time, since we took off from your United States of America. Ahead of us lies still a long journey, but circumstances have made it necessary for us to share with you immediately our motivations and our plans.

"We have been studying Earth and its peoples for a long time, particularly the experiment with democracy in your United States of America, and even more particularly the blot upon that experiment: the refusal to grant you full human rights along with its white citizens. We have watched your long travail, from the first slaves kidnapped into the country in your year 1619, to its crass and despicable acceptance of our offer to trade you for gold and other resources. That proved the truth of our observations: that white people consider you—as they considered you from the beginning—no more than their property, to be sold to the highest bidder.

"Ours is, as you have doubtless guessed, a society technologically advanced beyond yours on Earth. Yet astute as we have been, we have somehow lacked an element that you might call 'human.'"

The voice paused, as though before a profound conundrum. "Although we have," it then continued, "in observing your country, been able to make analogues of your voices and expressions, we find we cannot re-create your robust warmth and humor. We cannot re-create the emotional and spiritual strength whereby you have sustained that humanity through all your travails. We cannot, that is, re-create your ability to transcend suffering—to sing through it, as you yourselves might say.

"For despite our advanced technology, our people suffer, and we have lacked the means to relieve them. Or, we lacked them until, again after observing America, we thought that perhaps if we offered it enough of the wealth it seems to treasure beyond all else, it might be persuaded to part with the human treasure you and your people constitute.

"We hoped to bring you back to our home star, to be settlers there, to mingle with our citizens as equals and full partners in our development and growth.

"And so we devised ships to carry us through space to Earth and to America. And so we made our offer. When it was accepted, we were, even from our long acquaintance with your history, amazed. We now have"—the voice paused again— "another reason for amazement.

"We have been, in these two months, monitoring the thoughts of each and every one of you for any sign of illness or serious distress. And we find that many of you are inexplicably—at least, to us—longing to return to the land that you call home. That you long for this even though it is also a land that practices the most pernicious racism practiced anywhere in the universe—and even though it easily banished you against your will, sent you off to an unknown fate.

"It is perhaps indicative of our emotional ignorance that we assumed you would be glad of the opportunity to leave America, to make a new start in our world. But since it is imperative to our plan that you enter our society voluntarily, we are going to ask you to vote on whether you wish to do so or whether you wish to return to the land that has sheltered you so ambiguously these hundreds of years. If you decide on the latter, we will try to negotiate for your return.

"Before you vote, we must tell you something of what has been going on there in these two months. America traded you for resources that should, with prudent management, have solved its problems for the moment and ensured its prosperity for at least a century to come. Even in this brief time, however, these resources have been almost completely dissipated in a series of fraudulent corporate and government transactions. Now the economy is in shambles, the stock market has all but collapsed, and more than half the population is unemployed. The politicians, grown accustomed to using race to divert attention from their incompetence and corruption, are hard-pressed to create a scapegoat people to replace you.

"Furthermore, America's acceptance of the Trade has evoked the scorn and enmity of the other nations of the world. Having listened for so long to America's self-righteous preaching of rights and liberties for all, and then witnessed its willingness to trade away one tenth of its people for what they call 'blood money,' they are now hooting at it for its hypocrisy and its moral corruption. The United Nations are moving to oust it from the Security Council, and many countries have broken off all diplomatic relations and severed all economic ties.

"We wonder whether, knowing all this, you will wish to return to such a home. But before we ask you to vote, we understand that two of your number wish to speak to you. First, Gleason Golightly, once an adviser to your president. We know that many of you have condemned Golightly for his espousal of conservative causes and even more when, prior to the American vote on the Space Trade, he urged you to try to trick whites into voting against it by telling them that you, having learned that our star was an idyllic land, wanted to come with us. Golightly, applying his long study of white behavior, was convinced that whites would do anything to keep black people from gaining a benefit barred to them. Many of you, seeing his strategy as betrayal, rejected it; but, in fact, he was sincere, and his was the only ploy that might have worked. Mr. Golightly!"

"Despite our past differences," Golightly began, "we now find ourselves literally in the same boat. Because we are black, our history in America has been one of suffering and sacrifice, persecution and exploitation. Yet is it not precisely that history that draws us back to our homes and the homes of our forebears? To continue on with the Space Traders would be to abandon a civilization we have helped create, and for what? For a strange world in which we can never be more than outsiders, inferior by any measure to beings who control technology beyond even the wildest imaginings of our science fiction writers?

"Yes, life in America was hard for African Americans, as we all know. But as we all also know, my friends, America, whether whites liked it or not, is our land, too. For better or worse, it is our home, no matter that we are now farther from it than even those imaginings could take us. Our roots are there. Our work is there. There we have lived our lives, and there we have engaged in the struggle for our dignity, a struggle that—win or lose—is our true destiny. I dare to say what you are thinking: 'Space Traders, we appreciate all that you want to do, but *we* want to go home!'"

There was a murmuring in the darkness of a multitude of voices: some approving, some uncertain.

"And now," said the hidden voice, "you will hear from one who is among you by circumstances strange beyond even our knowledge. After you have heard her, we will ask you to vote. Geneva Crenshaw!"

"Mr. Golightly," said Geneva, "urges us to return home—but home, I ask you, to what? Given the turmoil there, as reported by the Space Traders, the nation's leaders might well accept us back as a diversion from their current crisis. They might even promise the racial justice so long denied us and those who came before us. Whatever those promises, we will have heard them all before. Whatever the words, they will be as empty as all the other pledges of equality made to us since the Emancipation Proclamation.

"At each previous promise, at each new commitment to full equality, we hailed a new day—only to find that the change was cosmetic, not serious; more show than real reform. All of these pledges have come to be one means or another to keep us enslaved without chains.

"No, four hundred years is enough to convince me that America will never change—indeed, is incapable of change. Think of all the times we have bailed out white America. As slaves, our forebears provided the labor for the wealth that funded the Revolutionary War. In the Civil War, black soldiers, many of them only months away from slavery, made the difference between victory and defeat. In war and in peace, we have been faithful, we have been patriots. But we have never understood that the essence of the racism we contended against was not simply that we were exploited in slavery, degraded by segregation, and frustrated by the unmet promises of equal opportunity. The essence of racism in America was the hope that we who were black would not exist. As Professor Patricia Williams put it, white America wishes that 'blacks would just go away and shut up and stop taking up so much time and food and air and then the world would return to its Norman Rockwell loveliness and America could be employed and happy once more.'

"Now, thanks to the Space Traders, they have their wish. Mark my words, if we succumb to Mr. Golightly's entreaty to return, we will find—likely before the welcome parties are over—that the nation will heap on our shoulders the troubles it has created for itself during our absence. Again, four hundred years of subordinate status is enough! Let us continue with the Space Traders!"

A stirring in the darkness was quickly stilled by Golightly's voice.

"I wish," he said, his voice breaking, "I wish I could guarantee that if we return, life will be different, that racism will be but a memory, and that we will, in the words of our anthem, '[l]ift every voice and sing,' till earth and heaven 'ring, ring with the harmonies of liberty.' But I cannot make such a promise. Nor would I have us vote to return on the fragile hope that America has learned anything from its double squandering: not only of the treasure the Space Traders brought them but of the human treasure of ourselves.

"I see our eviction from America as a cruel repetition of the abduction of our African ancestors. Let us not forget that those forebears—betrayed into bondage—not only suffered slavery and segregation but survived both. Yes, we all know from our own experiences in the last forty years that promises have not been kept. Yet is it not through struggling against evil that we achieve our salvation? Do we not owe it to our forebears, to our children, to ourselves to return to America, not as a further gift to an uncaring nation, but as a proof that we can—by the example our ancestors set us—wring out of present danger a life of commitment and service to one another and our brother and sister Americans of any color?"

I had to give it to him, Golightly was eloquent. Geneva, too, must have felt the power of his speech, as was evident in her response.

"Mr. Golightly speaks eloquently as the representative of a compassionate, humane people ever ready to forget and forgive. But we must be honest here. We are also a people whom trials and tribulations have rendered averse to risks, all too willing to accept the devil we know rather than take on the unknown, perhaps worse danger. It is this aversion that confounds the Space Traders and confuses us in this moment of decision.

"Mr. Golightly speaks of roots. Well, let us go back to roots. We, as a people, have always identified with the children of Israel, their bondage in Egypt, their emancipation by Moses with God's help. Well, we are not walking on the hot sands of the Egyptian desert. We are hurtling through the heavens in vehicles from another world, having been set free from the bondage of our American Egypt by the intervention of outside forces. Even as the Egyptians, realizing their loss, tried to recapture the Israelites by force, so if whites in America do permit us to return, they will be doing so not for our sake but out of greed.

"Did not the Lord promise the Israelites a home, a land of their own? Is He not now, at long last, offering us a home beyond the corrupting influence of capitalism, colonialism, and racism? The slave singers, bowed down and heavy burdened, sang of a City called Heaven, one they had started to make their home. Let us heed the message of their song. Let us go on with the Space Traders to a new beginning. To a home free of oppression. To a home where each of us has the same opportunity as everyone else to fulfill himself or herself."

Beautifully done, but not totally convincing to me. Geneva has, of course, a home beyond Earth to which, I assume, she can go whenever she wants.

As she finished speaking, a light flashed.

"It is time to vote," said the hidden voice. "We will monitor your votes as we monitor your thoughts. When the light flashes again, whisper the words 'Going on' or 'Going home' over and over like a mantra. Stop when the light flashes again."

Between the two flashes of light, I heard a sound, as faint but distinct as the rustling of leaves in a forest in a quiet breeze. Thus, the millions of people in my ship and in all the others cast their votes.

After the second flash of light, the hidden voice announced the poll's result. "Of those who wish to continue with us, seventy percent. Of those who wish to return to America, thirty percent.

"This vote is not as decisive as it seems," the voice went on. "In monitoring your thoughts when you were listening to Mr. Golightly and Ms. Crenshaw, we found that a considerable proportion of you favored whomever was speaking at a particular moment. Thus, we must assume that if Mr. Golightly had spoken last, you would have voted to return home rather than continue with us.

"Such ambivalence is very disturbing to us. We do not understand it, even though our study of your history in America has indicated that your commitment to that land of your enslavement defies rationality. And so it does. We are deeply disappointed.

"And now we have just been informed that we do not have with us all African Americans. At the time of the roundup of blacks in the United States two months ago, some hundreds of thousands either escaped to other countries or were successfully hidden by friendly whites. Some of those who had fair complexions passed themselves off as whites. These black people have actually been permitted to return to their communities, and we understand that most of them long for the return of their relatives and friends we have carried away with us."

At that point, someone began singing the André Crouch gospel song "Soon and Very Soon." Other voices picked it up,

Soon and very soon,
We are going to see the King.
Hallelujah! Hallelujah!
We're going to see the King.

By the second verse, whole hosts of people had joined in exuberantly, even joyfully—but had changed the refrain to "We're going to see our home."

The next announcement expressed a familiar exasperation—my own when, in the past, I had tried with little obvious success to get an important point through the heads of obstinate students. "Seventy percent of you are now ready to return. With every second that passes, more of you are veering around to that view. Indeed, your heads are filled with thoughts of home, as though it were—as one of your poets has said—'the place where, when you go there, they have to take you in.' But do you really suppose that America's leaders will invite or welcome you back?"

But, I thought to myself, what of the next line or so in that poem where Robert Frost suggests that home is "[s]omething you somehow haven't to deserve"?

As if in answer to my thought, the voice said, "So far as we are concerned, whether America wants you back is irrelevant. It is a sign perhaps of our emotional unenlightenment, but we cannot risk disrupting our more advanced world with immigrants who could not accept it wholeheartedly, without regret."

There was a pause, during which I thought I heard a faint sigh. Then a tremendous roar filled the space overhead and echoed through all our bodies. Somewhere huge mechanisms were shifting.

"We will circle your galaxy," the voice resumed, "until we decide what to do with you."

The ship settled into its new course. The only sound was Geneva singing the old hymn "Amazing Grace." Written in the eighteenth century by John Newton, a former slave-ship captain, it seems more than speculation that that melody may have emanated from the sounds of sorrow and strength rising from the holds of Newton's ship. As darkness fell, another voice joined Geneva, then another and another—all swelling into a great chorus as they reached the verse:

> *Through many dangers, toils, and snares*
> *I have already come;*
> *'Twas grace that brought me safe thus far,*
> *And grace will lead me home.*

2

⌒

TRYING TO TEACH THE WHITE FOLKS

I have never reached perfection, but I've tried;
Sometimes I have lost connection, but I've tried;
Sometimes right and sometimes wrong,
Hoping some day to be strong,
Then, I'll rise and sing this song—Lord, I've tried.
— Thomas A. Dorsey

Bong! Bong!

"With the sound of our sacred Liberty Bell calling us to freedom's task, this is the Biff Rightwing Show—the home of thinking conservatives. We don't pander: we ponder. We don't condemn commie-afflicted critics: we celebrate our conservative goals. Welcome, all you Yessirrees out there!"

Biff paused for the cheers and whistles of the studio audience, mainly middle-aged white males.

"Our guest this evening," he went on, "is an African-American law professor known as a liberal. He's got some ideas we conservatives consider crazy and some that raise questions worthy of debate. Let's get right into it."

Biff Rightwing looked down at me from behind his wide desk. I was seated on a too soft couch situated in "Tonight

Show" fashion—an arrangement better suited to supplication than to fair debate. "Professor, you're a black man who has obviously made it big, and made it despite having been born and raised in relatively humble circumstances. Early in your career, during the 1960s, you handled literally hundreds of school desegregation cases in Southern courts. You've been a government civil rights lawyer, a tenured professor at the Harvard Law School, and dean of the Oregon Law School, where most of the faculty and students were white. In fact, in a happier time of American race relations, blacks and whites would hail you as a credit to your race.

"So, given your impressive attainments, our viewers want to know why you, of all people, would write a book asserting that racism in America is permanent? The thesis of *Faces at the Bottom of the Well*—and get this, Yessirrees!—is that black people 'will never gain full equality in this country. Even those herculean efforts we hail as successful will produce no more than temporary "peaks of progress," short-lived victories that slide into irrelevance as racial patterns adapt in ways that maintain white dominance.' Now isn't that more nonsense in two sentences than you've heard in a long time, Yessirrees?"

"Yessirree!" erupted from the studio audience. "Yessirree!"

Then they let loose a chorus of boos, all directed at me. It wasn't easy to stand calmly before that sea of faces, all angry, all white. There was only one black man. He didn't seem to have a seat but strutted up and down the aisles urging the audience on. He was wearing a black cowboy suit complete with bright red boots and a ten-gallon white hat. Watching him, I shook my head. It is not unknown for subordinated people to try to please members of the dominant group, but this guy was ridiculous—and sad. I wondered, though, about myself. Is it, at some level, any less sad to be trying to teach whites who are obviously uninterested in hearing, much less learning, anything contrary to their deeply held racial views?

Then, as the audience quieted, I turned my attention back to Rightwing.

"Biff, my conclusion disturbs me as much as it irritates you—and your audience. But it is supported by current events as well by over three hundred years of American history."

"Pardon me, Professor, but let's stop leaning on history. Let's look at *now*. Let's look at *you*. You're a walking rebuttal of your thesis. If life was as bad for blacks as you claim, then none of you would have risen beyond being janitors, maids, and shoeshine boys."

"That assumption of yours, Biff, is one most whites are all too ready to make on the slender evidence of a few blacks who, in your self-serving, myopic view, have made it."

"Hey, Professor, you're evidence to the contrary whether you like it or not! You are black. You have undoubtedly faced your share of the so-called racial discrimination you liberals keep complaining about. And yet, through ability and hard work, you have made it. Tell me, Professor, why can't all blacks do as you have done?"

"Sounds, Biff, like a statement of belief posed as a question. Sure, I've worked hard, but I'm also one of the blacks this society permits to move beyond the barriers that bar uncounted numbers of black men and women whose talents and ambitions are equal to mine, but who have encountered one closed door after another. I grew up in a stable family and in a community that was relatively safe and very supportive. My mother didn't have to work and could stay in touch with my teachers. And every one I knew pushed me toward college— not as a possibility, but as foregone certainty."

Predictably, Biff Rightwing shook his head. "My advice to those kids is to look at you and go out and do the same for themselves.

"Now, I want to get to that story in your book—'The Space Traders'—where a majority of Americans agree to trade away to beings from outer space all our black people for gold and other goodies. Isn't this racial libel—or, more accurately, *racist* libel?"

"The First Amendment protects your right to call me and my writing anything you like, Biff. But that does not alter the facts about either the role of racism or the general understanding most black people hold about its importance to America. I lecture to many groups across the country. And when I ask whether my audience believes this country would indeed accept such a trade, virtually all blacks in the audience immediately raise their hands in agreement."

"Those must be some of the same people who cheer when Louis Farrakhan says hateful things about the Jews and other white people."

Biff's refusal to recognize that black people's distrust arose from direct experience with racism angered me. "Why not ask the Reverend Farrakhan to come on your show and explain his remarks, Biff? I'm sure he can defend them far better than I can."

"So," he went on, ignoring both my suggestion and my obvious irritation, "you want us to believe that the great majority of black people who hear your Space Traders story actually believe America would send them off into space for a mess of pottage?"

"I run into blacks all the time who tell me in all earnestness that were my Space Traders story real, they would volunteer to go. Knowing what they know, they say, 'Better risk the unknown in space than face the certainty of racial discrimination here at home.' Those statements shake me, Biff. They should shake you and those millions in your audience whose patriotism and commitment to this country's well-being you boast about so often."

"They don't shake me or my viewers. Are you shaking, Yessirrees?"

"Nosirree! Nosirree! Nosirree!" Their chant lasted until someone off-camera shushed them.

His audience's reaction stirred Rightwing up to a sort of religious fervor. "Any blacks who don't like it here are free to leave without waiting for the assistance of people from outer space. And ain't it a shame? Those blacks who tell you they're so disgusted with this country that they're ready to voluntarily leave—get this, Yessirrees!—they're still here waiting for *assistance*—there's that word again!—this time not from hardworking taxpayers, but from fictional beings from another galaxy."

"The shame is your willingness, Biff, to characterize and condemn what you don't know—"

"And how do the whites in your audiences," he interrupted, "feel about your assessment of the role of racism?"

"Some agree with me. Some don't. But when I ask them to raise their hands to signify whether a majority of whites living in their community would vote for the Space Traders' offer, most of them—however reluctantly—raise their hands."

"Not a very scientific poll, Professor."

"Perhaps not, but I bet even more of your viewers would vote for the Trade."

"And why not? Why in hell not?" Biff turned up his righteous rage button.

"My viewers are red-blooded American patriots, Professor. And many of us are sick unto death of your people's bellyaching even as you are committing most of the violent crime and receiving more than your share of welfare payments. You'd rather be coddled by wishy-washy liberals than carry your fair share of taxes and the other duties of citizenship. Considering all the trouble you folks cause, I'd be surprised if even thirty percent would vote against the Trade."

"O.K., Biff, you've set out some of the reasons your audience and most whites would accept the Trade. It's not that they hate blacks. It's because, in their view, black people take jobs from whites, live on government largesse, and commit crimes. Now, suppose the Space Traders were offering to trade for gold and other goodies, as you put it, not black people but the top executives of America's Fortune-500 corporations? Let's say that the Space Traders identified some two thousand of these CEOs as responsible for the loss of two million jobs in this country. That these CEOs had sent millions of jobs to third-world countries to get cheap labor and are importing thousands of foreign workers—skilled as well as unskilled—to this country to replace American workers."

"Well, that's ridiculous, and I would—"

"Let me finish, Biff. Suppose, in addition, that the Space Traders show how many of these corporations are firing hundreds of thousands of workers, many with years of loyal service, and all this so-called downsizing is not to cut costs, as they claim, but to enhance profits. And not only that, but these corporations are raking off billions of dollars in government grants and tax benefits, and much of the resulting profit goes to them or to those in the top 1 percent of the population who now hold over 40 percent of the wealth. So, Biff, with all those facts laid out, do you think your audience—or Americans generally, for that matter—wouldn't vote to trade away those CEOs?"

Biff saw quickly that my question was intended to reveal what his program and its corporate sponsors wanted to conceal beneath a nonstop attack on minorities, welfare, immigrants, and gays. Ignoring the thrust of my question, he used it to attack.

"That question should get you tried for sedition, Professor. Can you be seriously suggesting that the finest business minds in this great nation of ours are deliberately sucking up the profits of our productivity and keeping it for them and theirs while throwing most hardworking Americans the financial equivalent of a bone?"

"I couldn't have said it better myself, Biff," I interjected. "That's precisely what they're doing."

"And what *you* are doing is directly attacking the American free enterprise system. Shame, Professor! Shame! I know you have some radical notions, but not that you want to resurrect the totalitarian socialism that died in Eastern Europe, and install it in America."

"But, Biff, what's all the government's support of business and the rich if not socialism? The question is what will the rest of us have when all the good jobs are gone, and the government has shut down the relatively few programs that aid the working class while increasing aid to the already well-off? Where will your viewers be after the corporations bring the third-world home?"

"That's hogwash, and you know it! All talk shows are not alike. Don't confuse me and my Yessirrees with some simple-minded hosts, particularly that comedian Rush Limbaugh. We don't try to think and sit with the same portion of our anatomy!"

"Fine, Biff, so why not ask your listeners to tell us how they'd vote."

Biff turned to the studio audience. "What do you think, Yessirrees? Would you trade away America's finest business leaders in return for a year without taxes?"

"No, never!" Again, the lone black man was leading the charge, his "No!" distinct above all the others.

"Give me a show of hands," Biff invited, "for anyone who'd be willing to send our corporate leaders off to an unknown fate."

Not one hand went up. Biff looked triumphant, as well he should. Here, before my eyes, ideology was winning over self-interest. Trying to teach the white folks never looked so difficult. "Well, Professor, what do you say about that vote?"

"I'd say don't start spending your bonus from your corporate sponsors yet, Biff. A group's willingness to vote against a hypothetical case is no guarantee of how they'll vote when they finally wake up and realize that their jobs, their futures, are being—and always have been—undermined not by supposedly slothful colored people but by greedy corporate leaders. At that point, they may not be willing to sit quietly while corporate leaders are traded off, even for a year without taxes. At that point, they'll more likely want to tear them limb from limb!"

"Projecting your paranoia on our leaders is bad enough, Professor, but to suppose that American citizens'd be willing to send any group into outer space for money is too much!

"Now, let me ask you again, Professor, why do you write these racist stories? They stir up some whites and likely rile blacks into either committing more crimes or giving up on trying to make it in this great country. Why don't you devote your considerable skills to getting black people to pull themselves up and stop bellyaching about racism? It's just a sad excuse for those who don't want to get out there and compete. Why, all honest, hardworking Americans know racial discrimination disappeared back in the late 1960s."

"The public has been so thoroughly bombarded with the views you express, Biff, that the polls do show that whites *think* racial discrimination ended years ago. But it didn't! It's a little more subtle now, but no less oppressive or pervasive than it used to be. Just take a look at the polls of what black Americans think or at the statistics on poverty and unemployment. You and many other whites like to read these as proof that blacks simply don't want to work, but it's not just down-and-out blacks who know racism lives. Dozens of skilled and talented blacks told the journalist Ellis Cose about the discrimination they encountered despite ability and skills as good as or better than their white colleagues."

"It's an old debate, Professor, one our viewers have heard many times on this program. What's clear is that those blacks who are down should look for example and assistance to those who have made it or are moving up—you, for instance. And those who are making it should spend more time reaching back to help up their brethren, and less time either complaining about racism or—as reported in some of your magazines, like *Ebony* and *Jet*—spending enormous sums on luxury cars, fabulous homes, and ski weekends at resorts that cater to rich celebrities and charge accordingly."

Biff was well launched on a favorite theme. "And how about all that lavish spending by your people in Washington, D.C., at the annual Congressional Black Caucus Conference? You better explain all that, Professor, before trying to lecture me and my audience about the needs of black people!"

"I'm not here, Biff, to defend the few blacks whose excesses the media love to overreport to whites who look no further for an excuse not to be concerned about the plight of most blacks. My aim is to enlighten whites about facts the media are not interested in reporting: about the financial contributions and volunteer efforts of thousands of black people who are quietly lending their skill, experience, and encouragement to the less fortunate in our midst and doing impressive work."

Biff all but jumped over his desk. "They need to work harder, Professor. Black crime is on the increase. About half our prison population is black, a high percentage of black births are out of wedlock, and most of those children will live in single-parent homes. Where is it going to end?"

"These are all serious problems, Biff, but black people represent only about 12 percent of this country's population. I ask you the question that the senior *New Republic* editor Michael Lind has posed: Why do you 'treat the genuine pathologies of the ghetto . . . as the major problems facing a country with uncontrollable trade and fiscal deficits, a low savings rate, an obsolete military strategy, an anachronistic and corrupt electoral system, the worst primary education in the First World, and the bulk of its population facing long-term economic

decline?" Don't you think these issues would make some differ-
ence to how your audience—and America—would vote if
Space Traders offered to take in trade those Fortune-500
CEOs?"

Biff looked as though I had stomped hard on his toe. His
weekly program never touches on any of those problems unless
he can blame them on someone or something else: the trade
deficits on immigration, for example; or military problems on
homosexuals; low voter turnouts on citizen apathy; educational
failure on the absence of prayer in the schools; or America's
economic decline on the loss of moral values. Now Biff
repeated this litany, and his awful sincerity showed me just how
deeply entrenched all these false notions about blacks are.

Before I could answer him, he announced that after a
break for commercials there would be an update on the For-
tune-500 vote.

"And don't go away, folks!" he advised. "I want you to join
me in questioning our law professor guest about why he published in *The Nation*—an ultraliberal journal if there ever was
one!—an article that suggests we have a federal law to eliminate affirmative action, oust blacks from jobs they obtain under
that policy, and draft them into federal service at minimum pay
if they can't get new jobs on their own. Was he just expressing
some personal frustration at what he sees as the rock-and-the-
hard-place dilemma of blacks? Or have we caught an outspo-
kenly liberal black man with his pants down?"

Biff was clearly as intent on stoking up his audience as in
provoking me. But I was determined not to let him rile me.
Who knows, I thought during the commercial break, maybe his
resort to the old "pants-down" put-down shows some of my
points are getting to him? Still, he had hit on something that
was threatening to become a big problem for me. Geneva
Crenshaw provides me with great parables, but I'd begun to
wonder whether I'd lost something in my translation of a

recent one into *The Nation* article Biff had referred to. What I had intended was to show how much the pro–civil rights stance of the Supreme Court and the country has changed: now, rather than a shield against bigotry, the law has become a spear of justification for policies that undermine hard-won civil rights and threaten the jobs and well-being of black people. In my article I laid out an imaginary Freedom of Employment Act to demonstrate a likely ultimate outcome if this hostility toward affirmative action policies, and those minorities who are its supposed beneficiaries, were allowed to continue. Unfortunately, my fantasy had turned out to be so close to conservative reality that Republican congressmen were even now introducing legislation based on it. An outcome distressing enough in itself but also one that had stirred up my own civil rights colleagues against me.

At that point in my meditations, Rightwing—who had avoided making conversation, even eye contact, during the break—got the "on air" sign.

"Biff Rightwing back with you, folks, with an update on the Fortune-500 executive trade Professor Bell proposed. Of the first five hundred persons voting, four hundred and fifty would reject the trade and only fifty would accept it. Any comment, Professor?"

"Just that those rejecting such a trade ought to start reading the business pages of their local newspapers, with their almost daily reports of thousands of workers losing their jobs while the salaries and perks of top executives go up and up."

Ignoring my response and promising another update soon, Biff turned to my *Nation* article. "The Freedom of Employment Act you proposed in it is a conservative's dream, Professor. It's also, I'd imagine, a nightmare for civil rights supporters. One of my producers even feels that this piece shows you to be not only conservative but as much opposed to affirmative action and as supportive of involuntary work programs as some other black academics we've invited to the show. And she is not alone. The papers report that Republican congressmen have turned your supposedly hypothetical act into a bill they're planning to rush through before you liberal types can do anything about it. What do you say about that?"

"They're making a serious mistake, Biff. A law based on my hypothetical one would not only seriously harm hardworking black people everywhere, but it could arouse them to a new wave of protests and other direct action."

"All that 1960s 'take to the streets' stuff sounds far beyond the capabilities of a people as downtrodden as you claim black people are. Suppose, Professor, that, instead of pushing all this Doomsday-ville rhetoric and totally unrealistic group reformation, you joined some of the more thoughtful, independent-minded blacks who urge an end of affirmative action as a racially divisive policy that rewards unqualified blacks and penalizes qualified whites. Wouldn't the demise of racial preferences ease the current racial hostility among whites?"

"You may refuse to acknowledge it, Biff, but you know as well as I do that opposition to affirmative action is a way for whites to manifest their own justifiable fears about the jobs they're losing by the millions—not to blacks, but to technology, to third-world workers in other countries, to legal and illegal immigrants, and to the corporate mania for downsizing. Actually, many whites need affirmative action as much as blacks do. And influential media personalities like you need to tell your viewers the truth instead of forever pandering to their worst tendencies. They need protection against class discrimination that now gives preferences to those whites who may have inferior skills but get the jobs and promotions because of their contacts and credentials."

Bong! Bong!

Biff was clearly glad to be rescued by a viewer calling in. "Sam Storm in Macon, Georgia, you're on the air."

"Evenin', Biff. I want to know why you have a lifelong racial troublemaker on your show? Why, he's made a pile of money stirrin' up our good niggers, jus' like he did when he was down here workin' to mix the races in our schools. Now, he's gone to fomentin' class warfare. Can't see why you givin' him free air time on your show to do it."

"See, Professor, what some of my listeners think about your views and my decision to honor your First Amendment right to speak out about them! Is Sam right? Are you trying to foment class warfare as well as urge racial revolt?"

"I neither foment nor urge, Biff. Law teachers are seldom rabble rousers—"

"And, if you were, Professor," he cut in, "I can assure you that white Americans don't resent what you call class privilege. If they're working class, they strive to send their children to college to gain through hard work some of the advantages you see as exploitative. It is that attitude that has made America what it is. Some black people preach this form of self-advancement: Thomas Sowell, Shelby Steele, Justice Clarence Thomas, many others. Are they wrong?"

"More obsolete than wrong. Blacks, like most people, believe in work and self-advancement. But the economy over the last twenty to thirty years has denied more and more blacks the jobs that would enable self-sufficiency, much less advancement."

"I thought your point was that whites are also suffering because of the lost jobs."

"That *is* my point, Biff. In our society, work plays a three-fold role. It provides us money to pay our bills. It is also the measure of a person's place in the world and the foundation for one's self-esteem. Without employment, all three suffer, and suffer quickly and profoundly. But today there is a steep and continuing rise in the numbers of skilled workers—both white collar and blue collar, executives and professionals—who have lost their jobs and see little hope of replacing them at the same level of expertise, income, and benefits. Where—as you yourself asked a while ago—is it going to end?"

Bong! Bong!

"We have another caller, but first an update on the Space Trader vote. Seven hundred and fifty people now oppose trading the Fortune-500 executives and only seventy favor it."

"Maybe some of your viewers are reading the business pages, after all," I said. "Those seventy are almost ten percent of the total."

"Sounds more like you bribed some of your friends to watch the show and they've alerted their liberal networks."

Bong! Bong!

"O.K., let's go to John Luwanski in Milwaukee. You're on, John."

"My brother-in-law lost out on a job because the company said affirmative action rules required them to hire a black applicant, even though the black had less experience. Is that what you call fair, Professor?"

"It's no less fair than giving the job to some white who's a friend of the employer. And—as you and I both know—that kind of hiring goes on all the time. Or, it's no less fair than giving the job to a white woman, and white women are the principal beneficiaries of affirmative action programs."

I took the opportunity to slip in a comment about how employers use affirmative action as a convenient excuse offered to whites they don't want to hire for other reasons. "And, John, even if you don't want to believe that employers lie, aren't you concerned about the growing unemployment for *all* Americans? As I said earlier, corporate America's shifting thousands and thousands of jobs out of the country to take advantage of low wage rates, or using computers and other technology to eliminate jobs, or simply letting many workers go and requiring those who remain to pick up the slack by working longer for the same pay?"

"Don't companies have to do all those things to compete, Professor, to prevent foreign corporations from taking our business?"

"Unfortunately, John, corporations are increasingly multinational. There is no 'we' or 'they.' A corporation has no allegiance to its employees. It has no allegiance even to its product. A corporation's only allegiance is to its profit. And the easiest way to enhance its already handsome profit margins is to lay off thousands of workers.

"But, John," I went hurriedly on before Biff could interrupt me, "you're not off-base regarding the challenge facing corporations competing in a world undergoing drastic changes. Jeremy Rifkin is one of several commentators who have studied this phenomenon. In his *The End of Work*, Rifken asserts that manufacturing and much of the service sector are undergoing a transformation as profound as the one experienced by the agricultural sector at the beginning of the century, when machines boosted production, displacing millions of farmers. We are, according to Rifkin, 'already well into a shift from reliance on large numbers of relatively unskilled workers to a time when industry and even service work will be performed by a small, highly skilled group of workers who utilize automation in the production of goods and the delivery of services.'"

All the time I'd been talking, Biff had been twitching in irritation. When I paused, he exploded. "What a crapehanger you are, Professor! Tell me, does this Jeremy Rifkin share your view that the U.S. of A. is headed down the tubes?"

"Not at all. And I agree with him. These developments don't have to mean a grim future. The gains from this new technology revolution could be shared broadly, among all the people, through a shorter workweek and new opportunities for work on socially useful projects outside the market economy. But Rifken warns that the first step in any such sweeping reforms must be the acknowledgment, by those who represent us and those who set business policy, that private-sector jobs are no longer the centerpiece of our economic and social life. If we are to have a good and productive future, we will need strong, courageous, and humane government action to ensure jobs for all—perhaps with a thirty-hour week, so that our citizens have more time for leisure pursuits, for furthering their education, and for volunteering to help those in need and their communities.

"There is a tough challenge here, Biff, that economists and politicians have been, thus far, reluctant to acknowledge. Except for the poor and lower classes, unemployment is still relatively low, but it can be expected to climb steadily and inexorably over the next four decades as the global economy makes the transition to the Information Age."

"Come on, Professor! The free enterprise system has brought this country unparalleled prosperity. Why not stay on the horse that has proved itself?"

"Because, Biff, history has taught us that if the free enterprise horse is left to run without the strong hand of government to control it, it will destroy all. That nearly happened in the early 1930s—but the New Deal programs, while far from perfect, not only kept the country from 'going down the tubes,' as you put it, but provided us with much-needed stability and confidence. Similarly, after the Second World War, it was government that provided the G.I. Bill, federal home loans, and a myriad of other programs that not only helped to move us from a wartime to a peacetime economy, but subsidized the unparalleled prosperity you speak of. You keep saying I'm a radical, Biff, but all I'm saying is that now, in this time of great economic change, we need government again to keep people employed so that we can keep families together, sustain communities, and, in general, attend to the basic needs of all our citizens."

"I still say, Professor, the free market can do all these things better, cheaper, and without your misguided altruism."

"This isn't altruism, Biff, it's a way of ensuring that everyone, not just those who can pay for it, has access to the prerequisites for effective competition. Corporations, under the pressure of market forces, focus on profits in the short term and take no responsibility for any devastation—whether in terms of jobs, or the economy, or the ecology—that results from their single-minded obsession with profits. Effecting a balance between profit and growth, and stability and security, is the role of government.

"Holy cow! It sounds like the old socialism to me."

"But," as I suggested earlier, "isn't socialism what many in the top ten percent of our income and wealth groups are enjoying, those whose interests and lavish lifestyles are protected by the parties and politicians to whom they contribute so generously? I'm just asking that every American have the chance to share in that life—as is certainly possible in the current technological revolution. I'm afraid, Biff, that if we don't plan for everyone's welfare, America will inevitably become a third-world nation."

"A bit extreme, isn't it, Professor?"

"The Nobel Prize–winner Noam Chomsky and the Independent Vermont Congressman Barney Sanders don't think so. Sanders asserts that the United States is already becoming a third-world economy. Twenty years ago, America led the world in terms of worker wages and benefits. Now we are in twelfth place, with wages, health care, vacation time, parental leave, and educational opportunity lagging behind much of the industrialized world. In addition, twenty-two percent of our children live in poverty, five million kids go hungry, and two million

Americans lack permanent shelter or sleep on the streets. Food stamps are a necessity for ten percent of American families to put food on the table, and tens of millions more survive on bare subsistence, from paycheck to paycheck."

Bong! Bong!

"We have time for one more call, this one from another professor, Darwin Cavvers from the fundamentalist church school, Cross of the Living God College, in Southeast Texas. Good evening, Professor Cavvers."

"Good to talk to you again, Biff. I have two questions for my colleague. First, Professor Bell, you seem to resent what you see as the twisting of the race issue by white politicians to their own ends. Are you equally upset, as I gather much of the black church is, when homosexual groups—gays and lesbians—link their struggle for the right of sexual preference with the black civil rights cause?"

"I am, Professor Cavvers, by no means upset. In fact, I am proud that the struggle by black people for racial justice has served as a beacon for other oppressed peoples both in this country and around the world. Isn't it only natural that gays and lesbians, harassed and bashed about as they are in several parts of the country, should look to the black civil rights movement for inspiration, for tactics, and the courage to risk loss by standing up and resisting their oppression?"

"Well, Professor, I've been told that civil rights proponents can make for strange bedfellows, and now I know what that means.

"But I also want to ask you, Professor, about your prediction that race war, domestic chaos, and possibly a revolution could result from the transition in the nature of work. Do you see any way to avoid this catastrophe—other than all whites pleading *mea culpa* and turning over half of everything they own to blacks?"

I laughed. "Actually, Professor Cavvers, what you suggest

would be appropriate in fact, justified in law, and in keeping with the Christian principles I assume you and I both espouse. But, seriously, at this point neither confessions of guilt nor racial reparations—however appropriate and justified—will solve the unemployment problem and the domestic instability it is already causing."

At this point, Biff took over again. "Our time is almost up, but before we close, I have a final question. Suppose black leaders were to come to you, Professor, and ask, 'How can we get out of this mess—without either revolution or genocide?' What—in the few minutes we have left—would you tell them?"

"I would urge, Biff, that blacks continue with the many self-help programs already under way, programs that get only spasmodic media attention. You conservatives don't have a monopoly on preaching self-reliance. But you insist that no more need be done. That's cynical and wrong. We also need basic social reforms to benefit all Americans: guaranteed employment at decent wages for all who want to work; effective schooling and training programs; and child care to release parents to work. But, first, we have to make whites aware of such lies as the claim that these programs are intended to aid only unworthy blacks. And, then, we have to demonstrate to whites that these programs and policies are in their own interest, that they address a crisis facing *all* Americans, not just those whose skin is black.

"Of course, Biff, this message is fairly easy to convey when the danger is external, but our internal problems of jobs, schooling, and general welfare are as serious as war or earthquake, if not more so. We also need charismatic white leaders to drive this message home. It's a tough and risky job, and so far those whites with the leadership potential have found it easier to gain attention and political office by exploiting racial differences rather than by trying to resolve them. In pitting groups of human beings against one another, such exploitation is far more dangerous than any war or natural disaster for every single one of this nation's citizens!"

Bong! Bong!

"Professor, our time is up. Before we go, we have a final tally on trading Fortune-500 executives. One thousand callers oppose such a trade; only ninety-five support it. That outcome shows that my viewers don't think our CEOs are criminals. And, if they would support the trade of African Americans, that support would not be racist. Rather, my viewers are simply disgusted with blacks like you, Professor, who are trying to promote a radical social agenda using racial disorder as a smoke screen. In other words, you obviously want to toss out in the trash all the principles that have made America great. Well, we conservatives believe that America will do just fine if we return to traditional values, get government out of our lives, and support the principles of the free enterprise system.

"That's it, Yessirrees! My guest today was a black law professor who, like some politically correct Rumpelstiltskin, spends altogether too much time in an ivy-covered tower spinning tales of gloom and doom about our great nation, land of the free—and that's you and me, isn't it, Yessirrees?"

Over their wild affirmation—"Yessirree" over and over—his voice rang out, "God bless America!"

3

~

LIVING WITH THE
SPECTER OF CALHOUN

If I have wounded any souls today,
If I have caused one foot to go astray
If I have walked in my own wilful way,
Dear Lord, Forgive.

—Evening Prayer, Traditional

"Hello! Hello! I'm calling from elevator four. It's stuck on the thirty-seventh floor."

No answer. I pressed all the sleek buttons, particularly the one marked "Door Open." Nothing.

"Damn!" I muttered. What a frustrating end to my frustrated effort to enlighten a right-wing TV audience and its host about the realities of race and class in late-twentieth-century America. On the air, I had managed to keep fairly calm. Now, I wanted out of this building, to get as far as possible from that bland certainty that being white is enough.

"Hey!" I yelled into the elevator's emergency phone. "Where in hell is everyone?" Again, no answer.

More muttering. "I'll bet those sleezy-looking talk show crew people have rigged this elevator as punishment for my effrontery in not treating Biff Rightwing as the infallible prophet he and his audience think he is!" Then, I remembered that white woman who, starting to enter the elevator after me, saw me on it alone, excused herself, and backed out. Maybe it wasn't—as I'd initially thought—out of mistrust of my black skin, despite my evident respectability (gray hair, expensive suit, portable computer bag), but that she knew this elevator was heading for an interfloor breakdown.

After pounding on the door a few times, I resigned myself to a wait that might not be brief, and eased myself down in a corner of the plush compartment. The carpeted walls made a comfortable headrest. I took several deep breaths. "Oh well," I said to myself, opening my computer, "I might as well get some work done while I'm waiting."

As if on cue, there was a loud bang, the lights went out, and the cab dropped about two feet, then stopped. Now I was scared as well as angry.

"If this is that s.o.b. Biff Rightwing's or some of his fans' idea of a joke," I grumbled, "I am not amused." I took more deep breaths and started thinking about what I would do and say when I got out of this elevator–turned–prison cell. I thought of the many black men who spend most of their lives confined like animals, in conditions far worse than mine, and my panic subsided.

Anger returned.

Then I heard, from somewhere over my shoulder, an all too familiar laugh. I looked around, but I couldn't see a thing in that pitch-dark elevator. The laugh sounded again. It wasn't the comic's "Ha! ha! ha!" but a cynic's "He! he! he!" And I knew what cynic it was. Once again, Algonquin J. Calhoun was mocking me and my efforts.

Calhoun is, of course, not a real person. Never was. He was a supporting character on the old "Amos 'n' Andy" radio show, which was enormously popular back in the 1930s and 1940s and brought wealth and national acclaim to its writers, two white men, Freeman Gosden and Charles Correll.

"From its inception as a radio serial in 1928, the show," according to one study, "became a hallowed part of American family life, invading white homes that ordinarily might never have had a black visitor." Although a folksy wit sometimes materialized out of the slapstick, happy-go-lucky stories, mostly the characters played variations on all the most demeaning clichés of how black people were supposed to look, talk, act, and feel. For photographs and stage appearances, Gosden and Correll, wore burnt cork on their faces. They also went to great lengths to support their claims of the show's authenticity, including frequent photographs taken with blacks. Most whites loved the show, finding it both humorous and comforting.

And well they might. The characters were all varying versions of Sambo, for three hundred years the enduring comic image in this country. The historian Joseph Boskin views the Sambo stereotype as not merely a source of humor, but far more as "an extraordinary type of social control, at once extremely subtle, devious, and encompassing." Turning blacks, and particularly black males, into objects of laughter, insidious buffoons, served—Boskin contends—to strip them of masculinity, dignity, and self-possession. Whites used humor as a device of oppression. The goal was to effect mastery: "to render the black male powerless as a potential warrior, as a sexual competitor, as an economic adversary."

Even so, denied more positive images, black people accepted Amos and Andy the way many contemporary blacks accept O. J. Simpson, Justice Clarence Thomas, and a whole passel of black conservatives. They may not be praiseworthy, but they are still part of the family—even when they don't want to be. So blacks listened to "Amos 'n' Andy"—I know my parents did. We ignored the stereotypes and their likely adverse influence, laughed at the funny situations, and took comfort and a modicum of satisfaction in the fact that colored people were getting at least this recognition on radio.

In the 1950s, the show was converted into a popular television program, using carefully selected and highly talented black actors. Most were required to attend sessions conducted by white vocal coaches, to learn to speak like whites imitating blacks—to maintain the "facsimile of life" outlook of the original show. The black performers knew their roles were demeaning, but there was no other work for them, and many tried to imbue their characters with as much humane dignity as the lines would allow. They likely shared the pragmatic view of the Academy Award–winning actress Hattie McDaniel who defended her roles, including that as Scarlett's maid in *Gone with the Wind,* saying: "Either I can play a maid in a movie for $700 a week, or I can be a maid for $7 a week!"

The "Amos 'n' Andy" series might be running yet had it not finally succumbed to the constant pressure of the NAACP and other black organizations that denounced it as a continuing insult to the race. Actually, some of today's black TV sit-coms contain as many stereotypes as "Amos 'n' Andy" did, while lacking its cracker-barrel philosophy. And, of course, that's partly why Calhoun is laughing at me. He knows how we civil rights people fight hard to eliminate a law or policy we deem harmful to the race, and how we finally prevail—only to look back after a time and realize that the defeated government policy or law has been replaced with something different, but not better, and possibly worse.

Algonquin J. Calhoun is Amos and Andy's shyster lawyer friend. He is, in the stories, forever conniving and spouting half-baked legal principles which he twists to serve his self-interest. He is a loud-talking, self-promoting buffoon. Even his black friends do not take him seriously, though they are all too often—and too easily—beguiled by his get-rich schemes. Calhoun's credentials as an attorney are suspect, owing to his reliance on often extravagant and always nonstandard rhetoric and pseudolegalese. His vehemence in defending a friend or a client is counteracted by his readiness to retreat in the face of any risk whatsoever.

For blacks in general and black lawyers in particular, to call someone a "Calhoun" is to cast serious aspersion on that person's character and integrity. The civil rights lawyers with whom I worked in the early 1960s—Thurgood Marshall, Robert L. Carter, Constance Baker Motley—were all the very antithesis of the Calhoun stereotype. They were well trained and practiced the law with great skill and commitment to their clients and the whole black race. They were heroic figures who, I was convinced, would lead us away from the old world of racial segregation and, through law, carve out a new road toward equal opportunity and racial integration.

They are still my heroes, but much of what they, and we who emulated them, accomplished was all too soon subverted, as the campaign to get "Amos 'n' Andy" off the air had been. In urging the use of law and litigation as the major means to end racial discrimination, we acted in good faith. We failed, however, to recognize that even the most clearly stated protections in law can be undermined when a substantial portion of the population determines to ignore them.

Calhoun's mocking laugh evoked for me all the black people represented by those bleak statistics on black poverty, unemployment, crime, and family and community destruction. To many white people, including the Biff Rightwing audience, those data confirm their stereotypes of blacks as shiftless and unworthy of serious concern. The disregard for black poverty and need, though, obscures and desensitizes whites to the facts that two thirds of teenage mothers are white, two thirds of welfare recipients are white, and white youths commit most of the crime in this country. It is well known that the rate of drug use by pregnant women is not significantly different across race and class lines, and that drug use in general is as prevalent in the suburbs as in the ghettos. And yet, as the novelist Ishmael Reed says, "in the popular imagination blacks are blamed for all these activities, in the manner that Jews took the rap for the Black Plague, even in countries with little or no Jewish population."

Is it any wonder Calhoun is laughing? We have given him good reason to gloat. However grievously he misrepresents his influence in the law system, we grievously underestimated the depth of racism in that system. Calhoun offers to negotiate the white world for his black brethren, intending to cheat them if he can and to enrich himself. In challenging the white world on behalf of black people, we civil rights lawyers succeeded in assisting the society to rid itself of a policy of racial subordination—*segregation*—that had outlived its usefulness. At the same time, we urged the adoption of a racial reform—*equal opportunity*—that has, in this determinedly racist society, become a more subtle but no less effective means of maintaining the status quo of white dominance.

Calhoun might well envy the manner in which we, despite our best efforts, ended up advancing our professional careers far more than we improved the lives of our clients—and of black people generally. There is, of course, the difference of intention: Calhoun's intent was malevolent; ours benevolent. But given the similarity of outcome, there is no real difference between us as far as those who relied on us are concerned. I work early and late—I say—for my people, but any measurable benefits accrue more to my career than to those I claim to represent. All but the most pompous of us are willing to concede that black lawyers need to recognize a special humility as we consider the plight of our less fortunate brethren.

The question, though, is: What in hell took us so long to recognize what so many black people on the street knew all along? I thought of Jesse B. Semple, the Harlem limo driver who had brought me to the TV station that evening. When I first met him several years ago, he told me his mother had named him after the Langston Hughes character. While Semple did not go to college, he has more motherwit on issues of race than many of the scholars in the field. He said once that, for all our degrees and fancy titles, we bourgeoisie black folks—as he calls us—seem not to understand what ordinary black folks have known for a very long time. "What is that?" I asked him. He replied, "The law works for the Man most of the time. It works for us in the short run only as a way of working for him in the long run." Now, if Jesse B. Semple, limo driver, knows this. Why didn't we? Why didn't I?

I smiled to myself. Perhaps one answer is that Semple did not go to law school. It was in law school that we were led to believe that, through litigation, we could eradicate racial oppression. But our losses taught us that society's need for a scapegoat limits the reform we can bring about through the innovative manipulation of legal precedents. Lord knows, I try to teach my law students to recognize those limits, but those painful lessons make me hesitate to encourage socially minded young people to seek professions in the law. When I do, I try to warn them—though, I fear, with only partial success—about the specter of Calhoun.

I sighed. Getting whites to see how racism damages them economically, spiritually, and morally is almost impossible—as Biff Rightwing and his audience only emphasized. Calhoun may well be snickering over my ineffectual efforts to tell whites on that show—to say nothing of the many similar radio and TV interviews I've done—what they don't want to hear. Having failed as a civil rights litigator, I have managed a metamorphosis into one of the "new, black, public intellectuals." It may be intended as a compliment, but it is used by those who find in our writings and statements what they want to read and hear.

The effort to address the quite different and usually opposing views of black and white audiences is fraught with peril.

For one thing, as James Weldon Johnson noted long ago, a white audience's biases push black authors toward a defensive and exculpatory literature. As a result, much of what we argue translates into the forlorn cry: We are human, too. Of this unproductive preoccupation, Cornel West observes, "Black intellectual life remains largely preoccupied with such defensiveness, with 'successful' Black intellectuals often proud of their White approval and 'unsuccessful' ones usually scornful of their White rejection."

In the last decade or so, a few black scholars have been elevated by wit and good fortune to academic positions of security and a measure of fame. These African Americans are called on to perform what Adolph Reed claims is the modern-day interpretive role that in the latter part of the ninetenth century brought Booker T. Washington fame in the white community and lasting calumny in much of the black. Reed's assessment is harsh:

> As with Washington, the public intellectuals' authenticity is conferred by white opinion makers. . . . First, one becomes recognized as a Black Voice in the intellectual apparatus of the left, . . . one need not even put forward a critique that seems leftist by usual standards: secular, rooted in political economy, focused on stimulating political mobilization. After all, the "black community" is different, has different needs, etc. Reputation spreads, and eventually opportunities present themselves to cross over from the left intellectual ghetto to the status of Black Voice for the mainstream.

Many of those who gain this status do so after availing themselves of "opportunities" to speak out against black anti-Semitism, to decry black pathology, or to join those whites opposed to affirmative action. Blacks who decry racism, support affirmative action, and view black pathology as the predictable result of racial oppression are in far less demand as public voices. The public seems to enjoy debates between "conservative" and "militant" blacks, the more heated the better. However sincere or skilled the debaters, there is the sense of performance, of entertainment. The public is less informed than amused, more comforted than aroused. "After all, if even *they* can't agree on these issues, why should *we* worry about them?"

There is here the academic exemplar of James Baldwin's comment that a black person in America has only the options of "acting just like a nigger," or not "acting just like a nigger." Baldwin observes that "only those who have tried it know how impossible it is to tell the difference." Baldwin was, in his inimitable way, pointing out one more frustration in lives filled with futility. Somehow his articulation of our condition becomes cause, not for despair, but for quiet self-commendation. What he says is true, God knows, but we're still in there trying. For me, the best way to face up to and stare down the specter of Calhoun is to continue to bring my best efforts to those who look to me for counsel in the struggle against society's evils— evils that may be too entrenched to end but, however fearsome, must be opposed. For the black intellectual with access to the public, all is not ambiguity. There are models and measures that can serve as guide for the opportunities our status provides. One of these is Harold Cruse's *The Crisis of the Negro Intellectual.* Though controversial at the time of its publication in 1967, the book may be better appraised now than in that era of Black Power. Cruse, who saw the black intellectual's function as basically cultural, urges us

> to take to the rostrum and assail the stultifying blight of the commercially depraved white middle class who has poisoned the structural roots of the American ethos and transformed the American people into a nation of intel-

lectual dolts. He [and she] should explain the economic and institutional causes of this American cultural depravity. He [and she] should tell black America how and why Negroes are trapped in this cultural degeneracy, and how it has dehumanized their essential identity, squeezed the lifeblood of their inherited cultural ingredients out of them, and then relegated them to the cultural slums. They should tell this brain-washed white America, this "nation of sleep," this overfed, overdeveloped, overprivileged (but culturally pauperized) federation of unassimilated European remnants that their days of grace are numbered.

Suddenly the elevator shuddered, then began to descend. I pulled myself to my feet and watched the floor numbers change—not too fast, I hoped. At "L," the car slowed to a stop, and the door slid open. Outside stood a man in workclothes, the elevator repairman according to the logo on his shirt. As I started to leave, two white security guards accosted me.

"Whatcha doing in there?" one of them demanded.

"Trying to get out, rather obviously," I said impatiently. I'd been in that elevator some thirty minutes and wasn't feeling like being diplomatic.

"Don't get smart! A woman reported you molested her."

"If being black is molestation, then she may be right." I tried to shoulder past them.

"Oh, so you're a smart ass!" growled the guard, grabbing my arm. "Let's call the cops."

Just then another elevator opened up, and Biff Rightwing and his entourage emerged. I never thought I'd be glad to see him, but I was. I hailed him and asked him to identify me to the guards. "And please tell them that I'm neither a mugger nor a molester."

"Well, Professor," he said laughing, "I can certainly vouch

for who you are, but about the rest—given your people's tendencies—I'm not so sure."

I was torn between hitting him or quietly acquiescing so as
to get out of what could prove a nasty situation. Fortunately he
quickly added, "Only kidding, Professor, only kidding."

After he had cleared me with the guards, I thanked him
perfunctorily and headed for the street. Just over my right
shoulder, I heard the quietly insistent laugh of Algonquin J.
Calhoun.

4

∽

STAYING
"NO WAYS TIRED"

I don't feel no ways tired,
I've come too far from where I started from.
Nobody told me the road would be easy,
I don't believe He's brought me this far to leave me.

—James Cleveland

"Over here, Professor!"

After my long imprisonment in the elevator, I was relieved to find Semple still waiting for me. I had insisted that the show provide me with transportation to and from the studio. It was the least they could do given the aggravation I expected and got. Having Semple assigned as my driver was an unexpected treat.

"I gather you've been takin' a whippin' while tryin' to teach these damn white folks some sense," he said, opening the door of his Lincoln Town Car.

"Well," I admitted, "you've pretty well described what happened on that Biff Rightwing show." I told him where I was headed, and he skillfully eased the big car into the always frantic midtown traffic.

"Yep," he said, "I saw most of the show on a TV set in the lobby.

"Nothin' harder 'n tryin' to convince folks of somethin' they already know and don't want to admit."

"Yes," I said, "an awful lot of white folks are in denial about the real depths of racial scapegoating in this country."

"Blamin' everything go wrong on us black folks is a lot easier 'n facin' up to the real big guys. Must get to be a bad habit, like drinkin' or cigarettes. Satisfyin', but destructive."

I tried to explain that going on that show was a calculated risk. "I hoped to get some of Biff's viewers to at least consider whether it is blacks who are taking their jobs and endangering their futures, or corporate decision-makers."

"I doubt the good Lord could get 'em to see that truth." Semple shook his head. "My father used to warn me never to get into a pissin' match with a skunk. Well, I am surprised that Biff didn't take a flood of phone calls eggin' him on."

"The reason he didn't, Jesse, is that I told him I'd agree to come on the show to discuss the issues with him only, and not his hordes of admiring listeners. Even so, as you heard, he did take several phone calls."

Semple shook his head again. "You did better with them than with him, Professor. They don't think much, but Rightwing is, for all his redneck rhetoric, really good at what he does."

"Meaning?"

"Distortin' the truth, which is what you were layin' down. He twisted what you said into the 'white is right' racial views lots of whites hold on to for dear life. They talks about color-blind, but what they are is color *crazed*. Makes 'em pushovers for the Biff Rightwing types—which is why they fillin' up the airwaves. The best of 'em get rich and famous preyin' on white folks—which is their own folks."

"Or they get elected," I added.

"Yes," Semple laughed, "and they do that 'cause white folks's not only stupid but don't show much sign of smartenin' up any time soon. What we got to do, Professor, is take advantage of that!"

"Meaning?" I asked again, feeling Semple was somehow taking over in our conversation.

"I'm thinking beyond us tryin' to use reason to blast white folks out of their ignorance. No, we needs to use guile based on our knowledge of white folks and how they act when it come to race stuff."

"That sounds like the advice my character Gleason Golightly gives the civil rights people when they're planning how to oppose the Space Traders' offer. He urges them to spread the rumor that the aliens are going to take us to a land of milk and honey—"

"Yeah," Semple broke in, "I know the story. And I'd go for his scheme that whites'd be bound to oppose the Trade if they think it'd take blacks to a better life. But those high-and-mighty civil rights folks see stayin' the course as a virtue even when what we're doing allows whites to keep kickin' our behinds. And, since Golightly known as a handkerchief head from way back, no way black folks was goin' to trust him." Semple stopped at a light and looked back at me. "You, on the other hand, Professor, are a person respected throughout the black community."

I laughed ruefully. "Not for long, Jesse, not for long—particularly since the conservatives have exploited that *Nation* article of mine and, as Biff Rightwing mentioned, are introducing anti–affirmative action legislation based on my hypothetical statute.

"But let's assume you're right, Jesse—at least, for now—about the respected position I hold in the black community. How long would I keep blacks' respect if I really went in for guile? In the dictionary and in practice, guile is deceit, fraud, chicanery, trickery. Get my point?"

Semple sighed. "I been told Harvard messed up more black folks than bad whisky, and I didn't believe it—till now. All those years you spent there done taken their toll, Professor. Now, you lay aside that high philosophical bag and listen to me. I'm not talkin' dishonesty here. I'm talkin' 'bout makin clear aspects of the truth whites in their arrogance do not consider. I'm not talkin' about underminin' our integrity by lyin' or misleadin' 'em—though given the stakes and whites' advantages, the Lord would surely forgive some lyin' in situations like those we livin' in right now."

"So, what are you suggesting, Brother Semple—or, should I say Professor Semple?"

"I'll take good sense over a title any day." Semple laughed, then turned serious. "What I'm suggestin' is tried-and-true in sports. Like a boxer'll fake with his left before he throws a right—nothin' immoral there. Also, take football, a team lines up makin' like the play goin' one way, the ball is snapped, and the players all start in that direction. Then the ball carrier suddenly pivots and heads in the other direction. Nothin' immoral or underhanded in either situation. Am I right?"

"Sure, but what do tactics that are O.K. for sports have to do with ethical conduct and civil rights strategy?"

"First off, we got to keep in mind, lots of white folks scared of us and do a lot of dumb stuff because they scared. So we need to get across that what they plannin' simply gonna up the ante on their fear. Remember a while back when the Republican presidential candidates started urgin' repeal of the assault weapon ban—one of the few good things President Clinton has done? Well," he continued without waiting for me to reply, "all the liberals reacted by yellin' like stuck pigs. Claimed the move was politically motivated and publicly irresponsible."

"Which it was," I said.

"Of course, of course! But how many pro-gun voters did the liberals win over with that comeback? I'll bet close to zero.

Now, had I been in charge of the NAACP, I'd have arranged to hire three or four of the biggest, baddest-lookin' black guys on the avenue. I'd have taken 'em to a costume studio, got them rigged out in black pants and T-shirts with the words 'Black Avengers' 'cross the front. I'd have put big pistols in their belts and had some of 'em carry rifles. Then, I'd have made a commercial about these guys bein' examples of hordes of young black men who are disgusted with this country—which is the God's truth. I'd say that men like these can hardly wait for the assault weapon ban to be lifted so they can arm themselves and start avengin' the wrongs done their people—which, if not true today, 'll be true soon enough. Get my point?"

I had to laugh. "I got it, Jesse, and so would the TV stations, and not a one of them would air your commercial."

"Make no never mind, Professor. I'd get the same attention free just by goin' to the press and tellin' 'em the TV stations rejected my pro-assault weapon advertisin'.'"

"And if the papers turned you down?"

"I'd simply outfit the guys with fake muskets and have them march to Washington to urge repeal of the assault gun ban. I bet the repeal votes would disappear with every mile they marched."

"But, Jesse, such tactics aren't only dishonest and undignified. They'd also increase the danger of violence. The NAACP would never mount such a campaign."

"That's my other point, *Professor!*" I winced at his sarcastic emphasis on my title. "Too many of those folks would rather see black people dyin' than do anythin' that'd upset white people—especially the ones who give the money they now depend on."

I sighed. I didn't want to get into how reliance on funding from large corporations and foundations is likely to put a damper on civil rights groups' activism. "You have any other examples of your 'racial guile' strategy?" I asked.

"Sure," Semple said. "Take that Contract with America those Republicans laid down in 1995 like it was God's own solution to this country's problems. Just readin' it made me sick in the stomach. I mean, that stuff shouldn't fool nobody. It's nothin' but a contract on black people. The Republicans knew what they were doin'. They knew the real attraction in a lot of those provisions is they seem aimed at gettin' black folks. Democrats must have known it, too. But what did they do? Call the Republicans out on their racism? Hell no!

"The civil rights groups could have upset the whole damn thing if they had held a big press conference and announced they had discovered evidence that the Contract was a sham, a trick bag. That it was really a massive IQ test for whites sponsored by conservatives wantin' to test just how much disadvantage whites willin' to suffer in order to maintain their sense of superior status to black folks. Then, having got white folks' attention, the civil rights folks could spell out just how much harm that Contract would do to them as well as to us."

"But, Jesse, it's obvious to everyone that the Contract is a clear power grab from the far right."

"Obvious to *you*. You, and other black people who've been on the receivin' end of racism in this country, will see instantly that the whole purpose of such ploys is to be a sort of IQ test.

"And while we talkin' IQ tests," Semple rushed on, "remember how that Biff Rightwing called your Space Traders story 'racial libel'? Well, what is that *Bell Curve* book arguin' blacks' IQs inferior to whites if not racial libel pure and simple?"

Once again, I was struck by Semple's perspicacity, his ability to cut through the verbiage of politicians and academics. "I see your point, Brother Semple. You're saying that the Contract with America served the same purpose as Richard J. Herrnstein and Charles Murray's *The Bell Curve*."

That 850-page tome enjoyed an enormous success, with more than 400,000 copies sold in hardback. The book's thesis—

implying great social policy significance in the fact that black people score an average of fifteen points below whites on IQ tests—was no more than a rehash of views long ago rejected by virtually all experts in the field.

"Are you suggesting, Semple," I asked, "that the book was intended to test whether whites today are as willing to accept negative views about blacks—as a substitute for working out serious solutions to serious social problems—as were their predecessors stretching back throughout this country's history?"

"Yep—but 'stead of sayin' so right out, blacks and white liberals treated it like some respectable study they had to answer—like truth personified when it was really another sad-assed scam!

"Now, if I'd been asked to respond to that book, I'd have hailed the authors for their courage and urged whites to go out and buy the book."

"You have to be kidding!"

"Can an elephant fly?" Semple asked, as he pulled up in front of the NYU Law School across from Washington Square Park. "Wouldn't having the obvious victims praise the work take much of the sales-boosting controversy away from it?"

"Whew, Semple!" I said, getting out of the car. "You're tougher to argue with than Geneva! I'll be back in five minutes."

I was dropping into the law school to pick up the papers some students had promised to leave under my office door—papers they should have turned in several days earlier. Sometimes I envy those teachers who take a hard line: get the paper in on time or take a failing grade is their policy, and it seems to work. My preference for allowing some leeway is not without its costs, including my having to pick up late papers at odd hours and grade them immediately. Sure enough, the papers were there. I made a quick check of my mail, stuffed several phone messages in my pocket, and headed back to the car, waving to the guard, Sergeant Casey, as I left.

"Next stop is the Upper West Side," I told Semple on my return. "You're not leery of going north of 96th Street after dark, are you?"

"Not if you're not, Professor!" We both laughed. It's a trip many taxi drivers refuse to make, fearing that in Harlem they'll have a hard time finding a fare back downtown or—worse— will be robbed. The conservative writer Dinesh D'Souza tries to justify these snubs as "rational discrimination," the neutral adjective intended to cure the evil in the noun. His defense may comfort whites, but it adds to the rage of every well-dressed black when a taxi whizzes by only to stop in the next block to pick up a white person. Taxi drivers do it even at the risk of heavy fines, possible loss of their licenses, and despite the statistics showing that a high percentage of taxi robberies are committed by whites who give destinations in white areas.

As we headed uptown, Semple returned to *The Bell Curve.* "That book's bogus findings on IQ tests lets whites believe blacks got inferiority built into their genes, right?"

"Yes, but of course biologists and social scientists long ago rejected such views. There's no basis for thinking that intelligence is inherited. And, indeed, the very term *intelligence* is vague and can't be defined in any specific, graspable way. There is, on the other hand, in this country a depressingly strong and invariant correlation between resources and race, and between resources and success—including success in taking IQ tests. These are settled facts."

"You know, Professor," Semple said, and I caught a faintly patronizing note in his voice, "there's one thing that Biff Rightwing was right about. You do live in some sort of tower. Whether ivory or ivy-covered I can't say, but don't you see that all those settled facts are so much hot air to all the white folks dyin' to believe black folks dumber 'n them to begin with!"

"So again, Jesse, what would you have done?"

"First, I'd ask myself, knowin' they just askin' for a whippin' from all you liberals, why would these fellows put out a book filled with notions about race and IQ that were rejected a long time ago?"

"The easy answer is that we're living in a time of economic stress and anxiety, when racial hostilities always worsen, and Herrnstein and Murray were pandering to the market's readiness to accept such pseudoscience. Both authors are on record as believing either that blacks are genetically inferior (Herrnstein), or that many blacks are simply unable to adapt to the demands of modern life (Murray)."

"So, you sayin' those authors used outdated data just to make money. You chargin' 'em with lyin', but nobody wants to hear your charges 'cause everybody happy with *The Bell Curve*'s findings. So, Professor, if they lyin', they must know the real facts: namely, that IQ differences be due to racism cripplin' black people. But since they want to believe blacks inferior, maybe they decided to shut up their critics by buildin' into their computers all the disadvantages blacks supposed to suffer from racism—discrimination, intimidation, exploitation."

"Come on, Brother Semple! We don't know that!"

"'Course, we don' know it, but ain't it better 'n chargin' 'em with usin' bad data just to make money? Now, we don't know that either, right? Let's say they run all their computers with that racial disadvantage stuff built in, and they find—lo and behold!—that black folks actually score fifteen points higher 'n whites. In other words, they've found that black folks really smarter 'n whites.

"Now it seems to me, it isn't so much us bein' inferior that bothers white folks. When we really catch hell's when we act like we's as good as or better 'n them. Like when as slaves we learned to read, or tried to escape, or even talked back.

"Even after slavery ended, whites couldn't stand the sight of us actually makin' it better 'n they was. All that propaganda in that *Birth of the Nation* film they keep bringin' back showin' blacks bein' lynched to protect white women! It's a load of bull. It's when one of us had a farm that was doin' well, or a little business, or even a nice house we built ourselves, that's when the night riders struck. That's when the Klan came down!"

Many modern scholars support Semple's notion, as I told him. Paula Giddings's *When and Where I Enter*, for example, reports on the murders in 1982 of three black men who were lynched just outside Memphis for having the audacity to start a grocery store that was both successful and took away business from a white store owner who previously had a monopoly on black trade. That atrocity motivated two very courageous black women, Mary Church Terrill and Ida B. Wells, into a lifelong struggle against lynching. And historians like Eric Foner agree that retaliation against blacks who dared compete successfully with white men was the real motivation of many, perhaps most, of the thousands of blacks lynched during the latter part of the nineteenth century and the early decades of the twentieth: "the most offensive blacks of all seemed to be those who achieved a modicum of economic success." As a white Mississippi farmer said, "[T]he Klan do not like to see the negro go ahead."

All the time I'd been talking, Semple had been nodding his head, not so much in affirmation as in impatience for me to stop so he could get on with his hypothesis.

"So, Professor," he jumped in when I paused, "if I were you, I'd give those *Bell Curve* fellows the benefit of the doubt, and speak out loud and clear about how brave they were to put out data they knew was false in order to spare blacks the bloody reprisals we'd surely suffer if they spoke the real truth, and then I'd urge everyone to commend them for havin' real guts. See what I mean?"

I was awed by Semple's ingenuity, and said so.

"I thought you'd see where I was goin' if I spelled it out for you," Semple said, laughing. "Now, that Murray and Herrnstein would have had another reason to keep quiet about blacks' superior intelligence and ability. Telling the truth'd likely open another can o' worms. Think of all those whites who score low on IQ tests. 'Hey!' they might say. 'We not dumb! We just disadvantaged 'cause of our class just like the blacks claim they disadvantaged 'cause of their race!' So, instead of bein' comforted, whites would rise up and challenge IQ tests and other class barriers.

"So, Professor, rather than run all those risks, the authors went for conclusions that go along with what most people already believe. Better a book that adds one more libel of blacks as a people than raise a greater threat that could lead to racial atrocities and class warfare."

I shook my head in disbelief. "So, while we've been condemning *The Bell Curve* as a perversion of truth and a provocation for racial stereotyping, you urge that we should have publicly viewed it less harshly for what it is and more sympathetically given what it might have been. And, hitting it from that perspective, whites might more likely see it for what it actually is."

Semple smiled. "There may be some hope for our people yet if our spokespersons learn to use *mis*direction to respond to the uncivilized excuses for its racism this society so easily makes seem ordained from on high. And, mind you, I'm not talkin' about lyin' or no kinda deceit."

"Sounds good, Semple, but satire and parody can backfire, as I'll likely learn tomorrow at a civil rights meeting in Washington—but that's another story."

We had just pulled to a stop in front of my apartment building, but I was reluctant to leave just yet. "So, what's your bottom line, Brother Semple? You suggest that we find hidden aspects in *The Bell Curve* that will undermine the study's impact. Also, that we should express our view that the Contract with America is actually a vehicle to test limits of whites' readiness to accept the loss of their rights, jobs, and opportunities, in order to get even with, feel better than, and be superior to black people. And, finally, that this approach will expose the so-called Contract as a scheme cooked up by the conservatives to gain great power for themselves and their rich supporters and reduce most Americans to third-world status: poverty-bound, politically powerless, and infinitely exploitable."

"Couldn't say it better myself, Professor. As things are now, even whites who see the Contract as a fraud are not acting like it's a real danger. You know, though, the Contract is a test for black people as well as whites. For blacks and for whites workin' with us, it should be an alarm bell. We black folks needs to show we not fooled by all that patriotic nonsense spouting out of that Contract with America. We knows just how poor the social programs they tryin' to cut off actually are. We needs to rouse ourselves and work together to show that passin' laws like those the Contract calls for will result in challenges—and, yes, disruptions—that will add to the nation's problems. We've seldom been part of America's contracts, except for bein' bought and sold—but we have been the motivation for most of the humane aspects of the nation's laws and its behavior. It's time to rouse ourselves, to get ourselves off our duffs, and start doin' somethin'!"

I knew Semple was right. Indeed, his enthusiasm and forthrightness had gone a long way to ease my anger at Biff Rightwing. Still, the way ahead wasn't as easy as he wanted to think, and I asked him who would lead us in the action he had in mind.

He was so confident I wondered whether his car wasn't another ivory tower. "When we start movin', the leaders'll come, just like they did during the civil rights revolution, though—no offense, Professor—I don't expect we'll find many of 'em among the black public intellectuals like you. But they are there, and we will again recognize 'em when the people act like they's ready for leadership."

"In other words, black people, other minorities, and progressive whites must rise to the occasion one more time."

Semple laughed as he got out of the car and opened the door for me. "Seems like for us, it's always one more time."

As we shook hands, he invited me to bring my wife some Sunday morning, to hear him and the Sisters of Salvation Gospel Choir at his church. "We got," he said, "a piano and an organ, and I been singin' there for years, and if I do say so myself, we sound pretty good."

I was touched and delighted by his invitation. I told him I love gospel music, particularly if the singers are not drowned out by too many amplified instruments. Inexpensive sound equipment can be the ruin of gospel.

"I am with you, there, Professor! At our church, we use a mike only for the soloists, and some of them, I'm pleased to tell you, do not need it!"

"Sounds great! What do you consider your best hymns?"

"Hard to say. Oftentimes we sing what fits with the spirit on a particular morning. I guess, though, our favorite is one that fits our people's situation. All the gospel groups sing it, but probably the greatest of the gospel singers, the late Reverend James Cleveland, made it popular. Do you know 'Don't Feel No Ways Tired'?"

"I do, indeed. And not only do I have Cleveland's recording of it, but I even sang the chorus at the start of a lecture I gave some years back on Martin Luther King's birthday at Yale University."

"You didn't!"

"I did! Like you and your choir, it suited the moment. As I was looking down at the upturned faces of all those students— many more than I expected—waiting to hear what I had to say on that day that means so much to us all, that song slipped into my mind, and I opened my mouth and sang. Like this: 'I don't feel no ways tired.'"

After that first line, Semple joined me, and together we sang a whole verse.

> *I don't feel no ways tired.*
> *I've come too far from where I started from.*
> *Nobody told me the road would be easy,*
> *I don't believe He's brought me this far to leave me.*

5

THE FREEDOM OF EMPLOYMENT ACT

*If the world from you withhold all its silver and its
   gold,
And you have to get along with meager fare,
Just remember His word, how he fed the little bird,
Take your burden to the Lord and leave it there.*
—Charles Tindley

The preamble to the Freedom of Employment Act advises that
the act will allay growing racial hostility by eliminating policies
that undermine fundamental principles of fair play in a misguided and socially disruptive effort to remedy instances of past
racial discrimination, problems that mostly disappeared with
the enactment of civil rights laws decades earlier.

As introduced, the legislation contains three provisions:

First, it bans all affirmative action programs, including
preferential recruitment, hiring, promotions, or other employment policies, practices, rules, and regulations, based in whole
or in part on race or ethnicity.

Second, the measure establishes a strong presumption that
all persons of the African race or of Hispanic ethnicity obtained

their positions for reasons that included consideration of their race or ethnicity and thus were actual or potential beneficiaries of affirmative action policies. As such, they hold their positions unfairly and without proof that their qualifications were superior to those of other applicants who were not eligible for consideration under affirmative action policies.

Under the legislation, such positions are rendered "vulnerable to challenge" by individuals (job challengers) not eligible for affirmative action preferences and presumed harmed by them. If any such challenger can show that he or she had superior training or experience at the time the job was filled, the presumed affirmative action beneficiary holding the position must, upon formal demand, vacate the position within thirty days. Judicial review, after the exhaustion of extensive administrative remedies, is available, but the cost must be borne by the suspect jobholder. Jobholders who contest bona fide challenges, and are subsequently held not entitled to the jobs they hold, are liable for damages to the job challenger in the amount of job salary from the date thirty days after the challenge was filed.

Third, all those who held or were eligible to hold affirmative action positions are, upon surrender of those positions, required to find work within thirty days, or be subject to induction into what is called "Special Service" and assigned to work deemed in the national interest. The government, can, at its discretion, assign inducted workers to civilian employers with labor-intensive work deemed in the public interest, like environmental cleanup operations, farming (particularly harvests of fruits and vegetables), mining, reforestation projects, and the maintenance of parks and other public facilities.

The Special Service would be more like the military than the Civilian Conservation Corps of the 1930s. All those found physically and mentally able must go. The terms of service are for three years, except that failing to locate a job within thirty

days of mustering out results in an automatic extension of service for another three years. This would not be slavery.
Inducted workers will receive the minimum wage; and while
deemed on duty at all times, they will normally work eight-hour
days and will receive room, board, and recreational facilities at
no cost.

⧸

"Let's bring this meeting to order."

The speaker was Avery Jones, a retired lawyer whose civil
rights work in the 1960s had earned him much praise. He was
also the chair of this emergency session of the Committee of
Two Dozen, a group of influential blacks working in traditional
civil rights groups, government agencies, foundations, and colleges. The CTD included even a few corporate executives and
women. Indeed, as I walked in that morning, I glimpsed the
striking figure of a woman who but for her bronze skin was a
dead ringer for the actress Joan Crawford. It was one of my former students, Gwynn Gant. I was glad to see her. She had been
a great research assistant, and this was her first meeting with
the CTD.

For several years, the CTD had been working behind the
scenes to prepare position papers, litigation strategies, or legislative initiatives on various racial subjects for the use of particular civil rights groups or community organizations. We were
interested more in progress than in publicity. Indeed, some
members of the Committee of Two Dozen would not have felt
comfortable serving if their employers were aware of their
involvement in it. As usual, for this emergency session, we were
meeting in the Howard University Inn, a small hotel on Georgia Avenue away from downtown Washington.

After we were all seated and quiet, Jones bluntly opened
the meeting. "We all agree, I know, that the proposed Freedom
of Employment Bill is the most dangerous piece of legislation
in the Congress since the Fugitive Slave Act of 1850—the law

that simultaneously denied escaping slaves even a semblance of judicial process and endangered free blacks, whom slave catchers could and did kidnap and ship South. Going far beyond the elimination of all affirmative action laws and policies, this bill is designed, as its language puts it, 'to correct the racial injustices suffered by whites disadvantaged by those laws and policies.'

"The Congress can't wait to make political points with the majority of the voters who, according to the polls, strongly support this bill. And the President, who is always more responsive to conservative than to liberal pressures, has already promised to sign the measure as soon as it reaches his desk. Given his anti–affirmative action stance during his campaign, he can do little else.

"It is particularly important in this discussion that we adhere to CTD's policy of keeping in strict confidence what is said and acted on here. The groups we serve need our help more than ever. That help would be compromised if we were identified as its source. Moreover, I don't have to tell you that tensions are running high on this measure. The positions of some CTD members would be placed in jeopardy if our opposition to the measure became known to their employers. I hope that is clear to all.

"Now, I know that many of us have ideas about how best to oppose this pernicious bill, but for obvious reasons, our esteemed legal scholar member should begin by explaining to this gathering what prompted him to publish an article in a national magazine proposing legislation almost identical to that now pending in the Congress and, I might add, posing the most serious danger to every black man, woman, and child in this nation. Professor, the floor is yours."

As I walked to the podium, there was no applause, only a low, definitely hostile murmur. The few smiles and nods were clearly grudging. Given that I'd worked fairly closely on several projects with most of the members, their coolness was disconcerting. As I got to the podium, I heard Geneva's voice: "Don't take low to these folks!" Yes, I mustn't humble myself. This is no time for Mr. Nice Guy. On the other hand, I knew that this bill threatened not only our race as a whole but also the careers of many in this group who had gained their positions through affirmative action policies. Their jobs were vulnerable, and if they lost them, they could be inducted into Special Service jobs. Unlike much of the CTD's work, this measure struck close to home—a realization reflected in all the stern faces looking up at me.

"Before I respond to the chair's request," I began, "I want to make clear that I do not accept his assumption, shared by the media and many of you, that my article was the motivation for the bill we are here to oppose. It is true that both the title and the provisions of the proposed bill are quite like some hypothetical legislation in an article of mine written for the May 23, 1994, issue of *The Nation*. This special issue of that magazine was dedicated to the fortieth anniversary of the Supreme Court's decision in *Brown* v. *Board of Education*. I intended the piece as a comment on how much the pro–civil rights stance of the Court and the country has changed: that is, the law is no longer the shield against bigotry we felt it was in 1954, but instead has become a spear of justification for policies that undermine hard-won civil rights and threaten the jobs and well-being of black people. I was also trying to wake us all up to what extremes the current hostility toward affirmative action policies, and toward those minorities who are its supposed beneficiaries, might lead unless we organize ourselves to stop them."

"Professor," Avery Jones interrupted, "we agree with what you said, but why didn't you just stop there? Why add the fictional statute?"

"As some of you are aware," I set out to explain, "I like to use allegory and satire to expose and dramatize the real selfishness underlying current policies that are advertised as being for the good of all. This is an old and honorable tradition, going back to at least Jonathan Swift's 'Modest Proposal.'"

As the blankness in most of the faces looking up at me told me that my audience probably connected Swift only with *Gulliver's Travels,* I explained how the English satirist had in 1729, indignant at England's callous and cruel treatment of Irish citizens, written this short piece, suggesting that poverty and hunger in Ireland might be alleviated by having a certain portion of all babies born be well nourished for one year, and then sold as food. Swift wonderfully describes how such a policy would not only prevent these infants—children not being, he says, a "saleable commodity" before twelve years of age at that time—from "being a charge upon their parents, or the parish," but would also avoid "voluntary abortions."

"Yes, isn't it a monstrous suggestion?" I asked, looking down at the horrified faces before me. "But in his straightforward fashion Swift recognized that if something positive weren't done for the suffering families in Ireland, most of their babies would die just as surely as if they were cooked for Sunday dinner—and in much greater misery! So the fact that the conservatives have devised a bill based on my fictional one shows not so much that I gave them the idea for it, but that their racism is more extreme than I or anyone else here has dreamed possible.

"Now," I wound up, drawing a deep breath, "can't we get beyond how this bill came into being? Can't we turn to planning how to oppose it effectively, including how to turn disaster into advantage if the bill becomes law?"

Without answering me, Jones recognized Ken Whitfield, an oldtime civil rights professional, sincere but not imaginative. Always a nice guy, though not a fighter—good credentials for the job he has held as the affirmative action officer at a large state university for the last decade or so. Over the years, Whitfield had successfully cajoled and maneuvered his school into doing far more minority hiring than it really wanted to do. Yet because he did not "Mau-Mau" the white folks at public meetings, the school's black faculty and staff did not much respect him—even though he had significantly helped get them the appointments of which they were so proud. Now his first words told me that evidently this crisis and the all-black gathering had given him a new gumption.

"Correct me if I'm wrong, Professor, but until *The Nation* published your article, isn't it true that affirmative action opponents had limited their attacks to the repeal of affirmative action laws and policies? Wasn't it only *after* publication of your piece that conservatives in Congress introduced a bill virtually identical to yours? Are we to believe that this was a coincidence? Are we to absolve you of all responsibility for giving our enemies the legal ammunition to mow us down? For jeopardizing not only everyone here today but black people across the country?"

"Hear! Hear!" sounded across the room, along with a smattering of applause. As I waited it out, I heard Geneva's admonition: "Remember, friend, take no shit." I took a few deep breaths and tried to speak slowly and distinctly.

"Let me answer the last question first, Ken. No, I don't owe you, this group, or black people in general any apology. I've been working for civil rights as long as anyone here, handled more cases, taken more risks, and written more books and articles than anyone in this room. Does anyone here wish to challenge my record with their own?"

I heard some mumbling, but no challenge. "Now, during all those years, my work was accepted—sometimes even applauded—by you and black people generally. Now that our enemies have turned one of my actions inside out, you jump to accept the rumor that I have betrayed my own people. Your lack of faith is a sad commentary on this group and on us as a people."

Again, I paused in case anyone wanted to respond.

"How much were you paid for the article?" It was Claude Carraway, a pompous know-it-all in CTD meetings who—as everyone knew—was quiet and compliant in a series of nebulous corporate staff positions: assistant to this, special deputy to that. Those positions legitimated in his mind the impeccable suits he sported and the slight, but carefully cultivated English accent acquired, evidently, during a postgraduate year he spent at Oxford. Carraway's presence on several corporate boards had not resulted in any benefits to blacks working in those companies, all of which had abominable minority-hiring records.

He always seemed resentful of me, and I returned the feeling. Carraway (light tan in complexion, with hair longer than it was straight, a defect—as he evidently saw it—that he corrected by the use of Tuxedo Junction, one of those 1940s pomades) was a member of CTD because Avery Jones hoped he could obtain operating funds for the group. It was a hope that had gone unfulfilled, unless you counted Carraway's boasting about how much money he and his wife spent at fancy resorts and country clubs where—he dutifully reported—he was usually the only black person present. That his wife was white was his business, but many of us were dismayed by his frequent anecdotes about his children's being able to pass for whites.

I knew that Carraway's question was on many members' minds, and I made a big effort to put the matter to rest. "Unlike the fat corporate board retainers you boast about, Carraway, *The Nation* magazine pays very little for articles, and I usually turn down what they do pay me. Sometimes they forget my willingness to write without a fee, and send me a check for a few hundred dollars. I always endorse it to a charity."

"So, Bell, are you now adding to your despicable conduct by boasting that you didn't have the stomach to keep your pieces of silver?"

I looked at Carraway coldly and directly. "I suggest, sir, that you ask your mother about the condition of my stomach—and any other part of my anatomy you might have questions about."

He was not so removed from his ghetto roots that he had forgotten how, as black children of our generation, we disparaged one another's lineage by "playing the dozens," as we called it back then. Carraway knew from my look, my tone, my words that I was willing to fight. He stood up, thought better of it, and acceded to those who urged him to return to his seat.

"As I said at the outset, I am willing to answer your questions. I am not willing to accept your abuse."

People stirred and whispered to one another, but no one made an effort to chastise either Carraway for his statement or me for my response. I felt a bit rattled, but decided I should return to Whitfield's question.

"Think how few affirmative action programs there actually are that provide disadvantaged minorities and women with opportunities closed to them traditionally! Doesn't this tell you that repealing affirmative action laws isn't the real goal of those who are trying to repeal them? Doesn't this tell you that they really have another goal in this time of economic stress? And that goal is to arouse and encourage white hostility against blacks as the cause of that stress, so that conservatives will have whites behind them as they move ahead to dismantle social programs that benefit not only blacks but, in fact, those very whites as well?

"In my article, I was simply fantasizing about where such scapegoating might lead. I had no idea anyone could be so malicious as to try to turn my fictional bill into law. But now they've proved themselves so! How"—I paused to ensure everyone's attention—"can experienced civil rights hands like you fail to see the great opportunity this bill offers us?"

"Are you saying there's no risk for blacks in this legislation?" Whitfield interrupted.

"Of course, there's plenty of risk, Ken, but black people have been at risk in America for almost four hundred years. What I am saying is that this new risk also gives us a chance to take the offensive where we have been so long on the defensive."

The grumbling that arose indicated that most CTD members saw far more risk than opportunity in my idea, and I tried to set out more clearly what I had in mind. "You fear that many thousands of black workers will be challenged out of their jobs, and most of them will end up working—perhaps for many years—in Special Service programs in low-paying positions doing onerous work. The scary thing is that these jobs contain many aspects of slavery, the involuntary assignment to work that one can't leave, the likely loss of most rights, and the potential for lifetime labor."

"But, Professor, isn't that precisely why—if this horrific bill becomes law—we have to be ready to make an all-out challenge in the courts?" The speaker was Gwynn Gant, my former student. I was glad to see she wasn't hostile, only troubled.

"This is not the mid-1960s, Gwynn, when the courts could be counted on to strike down states' legislation designed to thwart desegregation. If the Freedom of Employment Bill is enacted into law—and it well may be, given the anti-black atmosphere that exists generally in the country now—it is quite possible that the courts will find it constitutional. And that is a realistic, not a pessimistic, assessment based on the unwillingness of the courts in recent years to recognize racism in its contemporary forms—although in case I'm wrong, at least one group should challenge the law in the courts.

"In addition, we should not ignore the fact that—as with slavery, segregation, and every other policy that comforts the hearts of many whites while burdening the rights of many blacks—the Freedom of Employment Act will, with some exceptions, gain the support of many people in both parties whose eyes are on the political prize rather than on the moral principle.

"I suggest, therefore, that we need to get statistics to support the common observation that white women have been the major beneficiaries of affirmative action, and then insist that the act cover them. Of course, the Congress will not do this, and even the suggestion will anger and alienate large numbers of white women. But unless they are included, the act's racial classification will make it vulnerable to constitutional attack.

"This, as some of you older hands will remember, is a variation of the tactic used by opponents of Title VII, the equal employment act passed back in the early 1960s. In hope of killing the measure, Southerners put in an amendment extending to women the protection against job discrimination. Title VII was enacted anyway, and it is possible that the Freedom of Employment Act will pass even with white women included—but I doubt Congress will be as willing to undermine women's rights as it was to extend them in Title VII.

"There may be other challenges worth making, but I would not depend on any of these efforts succeeding in the present political climate. And for that reason, the rest of us should try dispassionately to evaluate how the enactment and enforcement of the law will really worsen an already bad situation."

"I gather," Gwynn asked, "that you don't agree with our chair that this law would seriously imperil us all."

"Let's face a few facts, Gwynn. Our prisons contain—or soon will—a million black men and a growing number of black women. Their already miserable lives will not be worsened by the Freedom of Employment Act. Nor will it affect the millions of unemployed blacks. And as to those who are working, a great many are losing their jobs through the atrophy of minority-hiring programs and the downsizing that almost always burden blacks more than their white counterparts. None of these people will be affected by this legislation—if it becomes law."

"But, Professor, that still leaves millions of black workers at every level whose jobs can be successfully challenged by whites who, given the tight job market, will resort to all manner of schemes to get black workers out of their jobs."

"True enough, Gwynn—and these displaced workers will be subject to the Special Service provisions of the Freedom of Employment Act. That means they will be working and earning, and their free room, board, and recreational facilities will make their real salaries greater than those of a sizable number of whites. As more and more whites lose their jobs, those blacks in Special Service jobs will be pitied less and envied more.

"So, while civil rights advocates have focused on the elimination of affirmative action programs, neither advocates nor opponents have noticed the predictable result of, in effect, guaranteeing jobs to black people in an economy where jobs are disappearing by the millions. At a rough guess, it would cost thirty thousand dollars a year for each black assigned to Special Service.

"Thus, the way to oppose this measure is to focus not on its disadvantage to blacks, but on its burden on whites, millions of whom will lose their jobs without anywhere to turn. This act would, moreover, stir up racial hatreds that would almost certainly explode in riots and rebellion on a scale unprecedented in American history.

"In conclusion, we can contend that there are enemies of this great country of ours who wish to ruin it by fomenting fear, creating chaos, and spilling blood, and that they may be known by their continued support for this legislation. But black people and supporters of affirmative action, in general, are not among them. We should," I wound up, "urge everyone to join with us in opposing a measure that disadvantages blacks in the short run while it devastates whites in the long run."

I guess I didn't expect a standing ovation, and I didn't get one. The mumbling in the audience indicated that Jesse Semple's guile-based strategy had not won many adherents. I wondered whether I should have sent him to represent me.

"Any questions?" I asked.

Avery Jones spoke up. "Several of us discussed this matter early this morning, Professor. And while we're not really blaming you for the conservatives' use of your article, we think it will be difficult to oppose the bill effectively when everyone knows that your article likely inspired it. We would like you to disavow your article."

"But disavowing the article won't alter the fate of the bill!" The voice was Gwynn Gant's, and she came forward. "I think, Professor, you should go to court and personally challenge the bill's congressional sponsors. Under current civil rights and copyright laws, you can make a fairly strong claim that the bill is based on the unauthorized use of the fictional law in your article, and that you are entitled to enjoin the further consideration of the measure in Congress. Your position would be that their use, without your permission, of your article has severely damaged your reputation. More important, the bill's sponsors have taken a satire intended to enlighten and, without your permission, turned it into a legislative instrument that, if enacted, will do irreparable harm to millions of black people. We might also ask for the support of other individuals whose jobs and liberty this measure would jeopardize. In addition to an injunction, we can, of course, seek expenses and attorney fees.

"Winning would be tough," she finished, "but even the filing of a serious suit would serve as an effective response to the charge that the professor gave or—worse—sold the idea to conservatives."

The little discussion of Gwynn's proposal was mostly negative. The consensus seemed to be that I should make a public statement indicating I had had a change of view and now wished to apologize for any confusion and comfort my article had caused.

The chair put it in the form of an official request. "We hope you will do this for the good of the race."

I was shocked and told him so. "I have no intention of disavowing that article or any part of it. If asking me to do so was your intention, you should have made it clear at the outset rather than have me waste my time and yours with proposals you weren't interested in considering."

"We thought it best to hear you out."

"And let me tell you it was over my objection!" Claude Carraway shouted. "I know what you were up to! You were trying to pull on us the same sad trick your character Gleason Golightly tried in that damned Space Traders story of yours! And let me add for the record that, despite its popularity in the black community, I consider your story racist! Your fictional civil rights group rejected a sellout then, and we reject it in real life now! Some of us are sick of your trickery and tomfoolery, and we are sick of *you!*"

Carraway's speech pleased some in the group and upset others. In the ensuing shouting and name calling, Jones banged his gavel and announced a five-minute recess for the executive committee to hold a short meeting. During the break, Gwynn came over to say hello. As did Ken Whitfield, letting me know we were still friends even though he disagreed with me on this issue. Some of the people I had known and worked with over the years nodded in my direction. But it was clear that, at that moment, a majority of the CTD members saw me—and not racist America—as the more serious threat.

Psychologically, I could understand. The perceived traitor in the ranks is always more feared than the real enemy at the gates. I was, moreover, a more accessible target for their upset and concern than those who had sponsored the bill and were going all out in pushing for its passage and implementation. Even so, I thought long-time relationships and a career of accomplishments should mean something. I got concrete evidence to the contrary when, after the meeting was called again to order, Jones announced that the balance of the time would be devoted to working out defensive strategies, and that to encourage open discussion, he was calling for a motion that I be excluded from it. The motion was quickly obtained, and seconded; on the voice vote, a clear majority voted aye. Gwynn and Ken voted no.

I was shocked. Before I could get up to leave, Gwynn, tears running down her cheeks, chastised the group. "You're doing the professor a serious disservice. You should all be ashamed of yourselves. And, I predict, one of these days you will be."

We walked toward the door together. As I thanked her for her support, I heard—as she likely did as well—one of the members whisper to another, "Do those two have a thing going on?" It infuriated me, but I kept walking.

Outside the hotel, I was still fuming. "That meeting was supposed to be secret, but I'll bet the media learn about my being put out before the day is out. And given their desire to feed the public's hunger for scandal, more will be made of the fact that you left with me than that I was put out."

"I hope not, Professor, but if they do, we'll both survive." She hesitated, then went on, "There's one thing that troubles me, though, about your refusal to disavow your article. You have principles, and I have always respected them and you. But, Professor, we are both black. We make a greater sacrifice of our firmest principles, our deepest selves, every day when we work at universities, in government, at law firms, wherever. We do so knowing well that we're occupying a finite number of slots, that as long as we are there and the slots filled, even the good Lord would not be hired if He or She applied as a black person. Living our lives as subordinate persons means surrendering the right of righteous outrage just to stay alive—when we are stopped by an arrogant cop. For the sake of a modicum of civility with our white friends and colleagues, we stifle appropriate, even essential, responses to deeply offensive things they say in all ignorance, viewing them as compliments.

"Remember, you told me of your frustration when the faculty at Harvard belittled, in your presence, the academic credentials of minority candidates as obvious proof they could not possibly become good teachers and productive scholars. When you pointed out that the credentials they maligned were far superior to yours, their response was, 'But you are different.' You didn't cuss them out on the spot or"—she laughed ruefully—"talk about their mothers even though you were insulted—and had every right to be insulted. Most of them can't know what it is to be us and, not knowing, say and do things that challenge our integrity to the bone. I don't respond to each instance of this, none of us can and retain our sanity."

"Sure, Gwynn," I said, "we have to accept plenty of crap from whites—those who are hostile and those who think they're not—but groups like the CTD are supposed to provide an oasis of understanding for us who, despite our success, remain aliens in our own land. So I don't expect to be accepted by white society, no matter what I do, but it is tough—maddening really—when you are disowned by your own."

"I learned from you, Professor, that we black folks have long since disowned who we are. Life in this country is about re-creation of self with as much love and tolerance and humanity as we can possibly muster out of the hurt and rejection and scorn that seem our portion from our first yelping breath to our last gasp.

"You're a religious person, and the best of every religion is the teaching that we must let go of anger. We have to exercise our capability to forgive, if not forget. Forgiving at least opens the door for a later understanding or acceptance. It slowly builds that sense of honor we in this country seem to be losing every day."

My anger was now mixed with awe and gratitude. Present

and former students like Gwynn are a major reason I think law teaching is the best job in the legal profession.

"Thanks, Gwynn," I said. "You've given me some much-needed perspective, but I would rather file a suit against the real perpetrators in Congress than apologize to some of their victims, of whom I'm one." When I asked whether her law firm would be willing to undertake the suit she had suggested against the congressional sponsors of the Freedom of Employment Act, she said no, that its services were limited to women's issues.

"But," she went on, "you do need representation, and I'll provide it. In anticipation of what happened at this morning's CTD meeting, I've already discussed the possibility of my representing you. To be frank, my firm was not pleased to have me involved with a black man they believe has sold out his race. So I offered to take a leave of absence."

"And?"

"They turned me down without even thinking about it. I told them if you were willing to have me represent you, I'd resign immediately. And, Professor, you have accepted. I am resigning. No"—as I tried to speak—"don't give me a lot of sexist shit. I feel strongly about this."

"The suit is a good idea, politically as well as legally, Gwnn, but that's a very large sacrifice you are making in a very tight job market."

"I can deal with it, Professor," she said, smiling. "But," she added, her smile fading, "there is one other thing you need to know."

"And that is?"

"I'll tell you about it over lunch. My treat for all the help you gave me during my law school days."

6

~

SHADOW SONG

I'm com'in' up—on the rough side—of the mountain,
Just have to hold on to His powerful hand.
I'm com'in' up—on the rough side—of the mountain,
I'm doing my best to make it in.
　　　　　　　　　　　　　—The Reverend F. C. Barnes

The restaurant was in a quiet, pre-lunch-crowd mode. We were served quickly, and as we set to, I asked what obstacle might keep Gwynn from representing me. In response, she almost whispered, "Want to hear a story?"

I nodded.

"For as long as I can remember, I've had a shadow."

"Well," I responded gently, "depending on the light, don't we all?"

Gwynn smiled grimly. "My shadow was different. It didn't depend on where the sun was or a bright light. My shadow moved on its own, more the real me than I was. And it could talk to me—and sing.

"When I was a girl, my shadow was my best friend. Even then, I knew no one would believe me, so I never told anyone about her. Of course, sometimes my mother would hear me talking to my shadow, and she'd tell me it wasn't nice to talk to myself.

"'I'm not talking to myself, Mom,' I'd tell her. 'I'm talking to my shadow.' My mother would smile sweetly and say something like 'Say hello to your shadow for me, dear.'

"As I grew older, I didn't share the other girls' fascination with boys. All that incessant talk about them was boring. By then, my shadow was not as playful, more moody and withdrawn. I thought it strange, but figured I was growing up and, maybe, growing out of my shadow friend.

"The first time I lied to my girlfriends and pretended I was as interested in boys as they were, my shadow moaned loudly, moved off in a corner and just stared at me.

"It took me a long time to realize that my shadow knew that, in order to be one of the 'in' crowd, I was denying my true feelings, denying myself. Of course, for a long time I didn't know a girl had any other choice but to go out with fellows. And when I did learn about women loving other women, the names they were called and the abuse they had to take made me deny myself and my true feelings even more.

"In college and in law school, I tried hard to hide my sexual orientation, but it was tough. While most of the black women were complaining about the lack of social life, men were coming at me from all sides. That's why I hated looking like Joan Crawford. It attracted all manner of male attention—for all the wrong reasons.

"After a while, my shadow just kept its distance. It didn't speak to me. It certainly didn't play any games. It looked mournful, and it sang a refrain I recognized later as a gospel hymn. Do you know 'I'm Climbin' Up the Rough Side of the Mountain'?"

"I think all gospel lovers know it, but I bet you wish you'd never heard it."

Gwynn smiled. "No, it wasn't taunting. It was supportive in a strange kind of way, urging that I be myself."

Then she softly sang the lyrics in an astonishingly beautiful voice.

"With a voice like that, how come you didn't go for a serious concert career?"

"Well, I took lessons for several years and sang in high school productions. I recognized, though, that my talent—my voice—is a gift from God. A successful career is—as I once heard Van Cliburn say on the radio—a gift from the public. I saw too many gifted singers and actors, too, who never got the chance to display their talents. The public, as you're learning, is fickle. I decided to develop other talents whose use I had more control over."

"A good point," I agreed. "Tell me, though, choosing the law didn't provide much insulation against your fears, did it?"

"That's putting it mildly!" Gwynn laughed lightly. "It's one reason I welcomed working as your research assistant. I could hide out in your office. Plus, you treated me like a person—not a potential catch."

"But you never mentioned your confusion about your sexual identity—and we talked about everything."

"How could I? You were like a father to me, and at that point, I hadn't even told my own father. And, anyway, by that time I'd come to accept living as someone else while the real me lurked off to the side singing a gospel song. But then"—she paused, looking at me as though she expected me to know something about it—"I came out of the closet."

"When was that?"

"Shows how observant you are, Professor!" She laughed. "You were there. In fact, you were part of the reason I did it!"

At my blank look, she reminded me of the coalition of student groups that had rallied at my old law school in support of my protest against its not having on its faculty any women of color.

"At one point in the rally," Gwynn said, "a member of the Coalition of Gay and Lesbian Students spoke about the difficulties of gayness. She understood, she said, why people remained in the closet, but their invisibility came at a terrible price—self-denial. She summoned the gay and lesbian students to come forward on their own to take a stand. First, other members of the group formed a line behind the speaker. Then, slowly, other students—who had until that very moment kept secret their sexual orientation—came forward and joined hands with the COGLS members. On the spur of the moment, I pushed through the crowd and linked my arms with theirs. Everyone was moved, tears were flowing, and the students were applauding and cheering."

As she spoke, I recalled the rally and Gwynn's joining the group. "But," I said, "I thought you all were heterosexual students showing solidarity with the gay and lesbian group."

"You were probably the only one who thought that, Professor, but that's the way it should be. It shouldn't be a big deal but, of course, it is. Acknowledging that I was a lesbian lifted a great burden, one I was glad to be free of. But"—she laughed ruefully—"it brought several new ones in its place. Friends dropped out of my life as though I'd contracted some dread disease, and some of the men who'd been panting after me now barely knew my name, and few would look me in the eye. And after law school, you can't imagine the jobs I didn't get, the apartment leases that were terminated!"

Gwynn's voice broke, and she paused to sip her coffee, her hand trembling slightly as she lifted the cup. I waited until she had collected herself. "You know," she went on, "the toughest part was dealing with lots of folks in the black community, including any number of my black sisters. When I was shunned by whites, I considered it part of the price of being black. When my own turned their backs on me for reasons no better than those motivating white hostility, it was tough. Lesbian baiting in the black community is not as bad as it once was, but it's still present and tends to obscure the serious levels of racism and sexism we face. Oh, I understand some of the psychology. Our difference enables the oppressed to become the oppressor. In fact, it is a sexual difference to which people react with a hostility based on fear, as they did this morning to your political difference. All too many black men and heterosexual black women succumb to the temptation as though we are the threat, when we need to save our energies for our true enemies."

"I would guess, Gwynn, that part of your burden is dealing with those who, far from hostile, consider their advice and suggestions as needed to put you back on the right and righteous path. If you're a lesbian and particularly if you're up front about it, you have an addiction—like alcoholism or gambling—and you need professional counsel and lots and lots of prayer."

Gwynn smiled wearily. "Particularly, the prayer. I've had perfect strangers come up to me and quote the Bible as proof of my sin and certain damnation."

I was well aware how dangerous the Bible can become when people view it as literal truth rather than as inspirational message. I mentioned to Gwynn an article in *Essence* magazine by Linda Villarosa, the executive editor, in which she analyzes the scriptural passages that seem to condemn homosexuality.

"Not only did Villarosa find some clear misinterpretations, but those passages that seem to ban same-sex love also ban a lot of other activities that are ignored by those who selectively quote the Bible to support their own prejudices."

"Yes," Gwynn said, her eyes shining, "Villarosa has more courage than most of us. She has not only written about her life as an African-American lesbian, but actually goes out lecturing about her experiences and what she has learned. She really catches it!"

"I'll say!" I told Gwynn about an incident at one of Villarosa's lectures. As she reported it in her *Essence* article, a black woman in her mid-thirties—turned out in an elegant business suit, bright gold jewelry, and her hair done up in braided extensions—got up and related how she had been attracted to women earlier in her life, but now she had found Jesus Christ and come to realize from reading her Bible that homosexuality is unnatural and those who practice it will be condemned as sinners. Taking out her Bible, she quoted verses 26 and 27 from the first chapter of Romans, which are often cited as proof of God's disgust for men and women who give up natural man-woman relations for "shameless acts" of unnatural man-man and woman-woman relationships.

"And," Gwynn said with resignation, "every person who quotes that passage thinks you've never heard it before."

"Well, Villarosa had heard it and was prepared. Reaching for her own Bible, she quoted from 1 Timothy, chapter 2, verse 9: 'The women should adorn themselves modestly and sensibly in seemly apparel, not with braided hair or gold or pearls or costly attire.' The beautifully turned-out woman—with her expensive suit, braided hair, and gold jewelry—looked confused and angry, and charged Villarosa with taking the Bible out of context. 'But that's what you have been doing,' Villarosa responded."

"Right on, sister!" Gwynn looked triumphant. "I can't tell you how much insight and support I've gained from Villarosa, as well as from the writings of other women, like Audre Lorde, Dionne Brand, Sarah Schulman, who are willing to speak out about discrimination that, while devastating, is not—with a few exceptions—prohibited by law.

"Of course," she added, "the extension of civil rights laws to cover sexual orientation will offer little protection against the anti-lesbian hysteria of many black men."

"The Supreme Court isn't much help either," I ventured, "refusing, in 1986, to do what they'll have to do eventually—acknowledge that homosexuals are an identifiable group suffering discrimination because of innate characteristics that entitle them to special protection of their basic rights."

"You seem awfully certain about that, given the Court's intransigence on the issue."

"That's certainly true for the present, but I think that as more and more lesbian and gay persons want to buy and sell property together, marry, have or adopt children, make wills, and carry out all the aspects of life controlled by legal rules, the law will have to recognize and encompass these transactions. It's already happening with the enactment of 'partnership laws' in many places where there is no recognition of homosexual civil rights."

"You're only saying that, Professor, because the law abhors a vacuum. It will fill the need for our property transactions, but won't recognize our different sexual needs that give rise to those property transactions. Small comfort, I must say! And, don't forget, the few gay and lesbian civil rights statutes now on the books are under attack—in Colorado and elsewhere."

"I'm certainly not saying there's no problem, Gwynn, but it's far from hopeless. And the continuing hostility in some segments of the public is certainly no reason not to have you represent me in the suit against Congress. I may be old and out of touch, but in the more than a quarter of a century I've been teaching law, I've had a goodly number of openly gay and lesbian students. Knowing them as students and then friends has simply confirmed my conviction that sexual preference is a personal matter. Those not involved should stay out of it."

"That's fine for you, Professor. But you and I both know the world out there, particularly the black community, is not at all tolerant of gays and lesbians. Given the troubles you're facing, are you sure you want to risk taking on this issue, too?"

"Look who's talking about troubles! Here you are black, a woman, and openly lesbian, and yet you're still fighting and willing to do publicly what you did privately in that Committee of Two Dozen meeting this morning, and come to the defense of a most unpopular brother. Yes, Gwynn, I absolutely want you to represent me! You're a good lawyer and a very savvy person, just the one to have on my side. Is that clear?"

"You're a nice man, Professor, but—" Gwynn's hard look told me that she found me wanting in a certain shrewdness, as Geneva sometimes did. "If we go ahead with that lawsuit against the congressional sponsors of the Freedom of Employment Bill, I'm not sure you really know what you're in for. They have lots of clout, and people, particularly a lot of black people, will try to do you in for a little bit of money—and I do mean, relatively speaking, a little bit. So get ready for all manner of gratuitous attacks—including insinuations that we're going together, like we heard this morning—just because I stood up for you and left after they put you out. Or, some will suggest that your hiring me, a lesbian, as your lawyer proves you must be gay yourself. How are you going to respond in a press conference when one of the tabloid reporters asks you if you're gay?"

"I'd answer, 'My sexual preference is entirely my business. It has nothing to do with the issues. Let's stick to them.'

"And, as for betrayals by some blacks, Gwynn, we know what our own did to Martin Luther King when he broadened his criticism of racial injustice to include economic injustice and the unjust war in Vietnam. Malcolm X was killed when his criticism of America's hypocrisy about race began to include what he deemed hypocrisy within the Muslim leadership. And Paul Robeson was abandoned by black leaders for speaking the truth about racism in the middle of the post–World War II fear of communism. I'm not anywhere in the league of these great men. So I'll try to get ready for some real betrayals by those charging me with betrayal."

I had hoped to put Gwynn's mind at rest, but she just nodded and kept on toying with her coffee cup. What could be bothering her? "So," I asked, striving for lightness, "is my black lesbian lawyer telling me she has her personal life in order and is ready and able to work full-time on my case?"

She darted a quick glance at me, then asked, "I wonder whether any of us ever gets our lives truly in order?"

Then she sank again deep into some private concern. I felt the best thing for me to do was to wait for her to reveal her trouble in her own time. Finally she did.

"You said earlier that I'm a fighter. Well, I try, but it's been hard. Last night, I told my companion both that I expected there'd be a lot of hostility against you at the CTD meeting, and that I planned to stand up for you and defend you. She and I had quite an argument."

I thought a moment. "One guess. The fight was about your representing me, losing your job—and income—as a result, and expecting that she would support you financially as well as emotionally until you pull things together. Right?"

Her look conveyed some surprise and a lot of thanks.

"How did you know?"

"I didn't. But when I feel deeply about something, something for which I'm ready to take a substantial risk, I treat my loved ones as though they are me and thus entirely ready to do what I've decided on. This, of course, is crazy and selfish. It can lead to all kinds of trouble. Whether partner or spouse, you have to get some agreement on issues—especially these—for which you're ready to take on the whole world."

"Right again!" Then she sighed. "There's one more thing." Another sigh. Finally, she got it out. "My companion, Meredith, is white."

"And?"

"She can't see why I should be risking my career and our relationship all for one black man, as she put it."

"She may be right."

"She's not, and you know it. What they're trying to do to

you is what this society has done—or tried to do—to every black man who has stood up for the race or for his rights since 1770 when Crispus Attucks, a runaway slave, was the first man to fall at the Boston Massacre. And every black person who hears what happened to Attucks knows it was no accident the British got him first."

"That's going back pretty far, Gwynn, particularly when you know that Attucks led the protest against the presence of British soldiers in Boston, shouting, 'The way to get rid of these soldiers is to attack the main guard.'"

"Of course, we don't *really* know that the soldiers aimed at Attucks because he was black. It's just that our experience in this racist country makes us *think* we really know. It's black people's racial insight I miss with Meredith. *You* know. We hear that an undercover subway cop has been shot four times by an off-duty policeman who thought he was halting a robbery—"

"And," I interrupted, "all black people know before the authorities finally release all the facts that the undercover cop was black and the one who went crazy and kept shooting after the so-called suspect was down was white. Right?"

"Precisely!"

"A shared paranoia, Gwynn, isn't necessarily something to be proud of. It also causes us to condone black behavior we should condemn."

"It's like a battle scar. Sure, it hurts sometime when it shouldn't, but it's also painful, even paranoid proof you've learned how to survive as an outsider in a country forever boasting of its inclusiveness."

"I assume your Meredith has the scars of her lesbianism?"

"True enough. And I just took it for granted that our understanding in one important area of our lives—sex—where we're outsiders would also cover at least the main parts of another area: race. But I realized last night that Meredith can never understand what it is to be black in America."

"You're certainly right about many whites, but we both know white people who do come to understand—at least as well as some of our own."

Gwynn shook her head. "It's true," I assured her. "What you have to remember, Gwynn, is that you've brought Meredith into a life, yours, that in many ways is like taking her to another country, one where she doesn't know the language, the rituals, the customs, nothing."

I paused to consider how to put it. "Sure, most Americans are white, and Meredith is white. In that sense, she is home. But you are taking her to a foreign shore with no delineated boundaries."

"Oh, Professor, don't side with her! Had I taken her to another country, everything would be fine. It's here at home where whites have almost no empathy for blacks as a people. Whites can deal with, even come to love individual blacks, but only if they separate the individual from the mass. 'You're different' is no compliment when you're being distinguished from your people."

"O.K., Meredith is at home, Gwynn, but it's home on the other side of the looking glass. Everything is reversed, back to front. She doesn't realize what's happening. You do. So if you love her, it's your responsibility to teach her. She can learn, as we did, the psalms of survival when home is an alien land."

Gwynn took a deep breath and let it escape very slowly. "Maybe. Maybe. I don't know. Right now, I don't care. Love is out there. My work is right here. Love in the absence of work can't survive."

"Hmm. An interesting variation on the Biblical reminder that '[f]aith without works is dead.' But doesn't Shakespeare urge that 'love is not love/Which alters when it alteration finds,/Or bends with the remover to remove'?"

"I'm too old," Gwynn protested, "for all that business about love's being 'an ever-fixed mark,/That looks on tempests and is never shaken.'" And she laughed as she capped my quote from Shakespeare's Sonnet 116. "That's denial," she went on, "and I'm too old for denial, too. Audre Lorde has written of the separation she felt from her white lover: 'Over time I came to realize that it colored our perceptions and made a difference in the ways I saw pieces of the worlds we shared.' Lorde was willing 'to deal with that difference outside of [her] relationship,' to let it be her 'own secret knowledge,' her 'own secret pain.' But I'm not!"

Gwynn smiled at last and moved her empty cup out of reach. "My shadow is me now," she said, patting herself on the chest, "and I am it." She began to hum, "'I'm com'in' up—on the rough side—of the mountain.' That's what I like to sing," she added, "when I'm trying to cope with some racial or sexual problem."

I reached out my hand to Gwynn. "You know," I said, "the rough side is the only way you can climb a mountain. On the smooth side, there are no footholds, nothing to grab on to. So, the hard way, the rough way, is the only way."

7

⁓

THE MENTALITY
OF RACE

Courage my soul, and let us journey on,
Tho' the night is dark it won't be very long,
Thanks be to God, the morning light appears,
And the storm is passing over, Hallelujah!
—Charles A. Tindley

Concern for Gwynn Gant's problems had pushed my anger away. On the plane ride back to New York, it returned. How could a group of black people—my peers, and many my junior by two decades or more—have actually asked me to leave their meeting? Disagreeing with the wisdom of my story was one thing. Banishing me as a spy for white conservatives was an outrage. Back in New York, though it was early evening, I went to my office. As soon as I walked in, I turned on my radio, and learned that all the major black civil rights figures had gotten together to condemn my hypothetical Freedom of Employment Act article as an open invitation to place blacks into forced labor. Claiming that I was betraying all black people, a member of the group, who spoke only on condition of anonymity, said he understood on good authority that I had been paid thousands of dollars to write and publish *The Nation* article.

"Damn!" I said to myself. I knew the source of that bit of misinformation: Claude Carraway! Gwynn had asked me to forgive the CTD members, including him, but even the good Lord might not forgive out-and-out hypocrisy.

"Damn!" I repeated. It takes real talent to alienate simultaneously the far right and the moderates in civil rights. My wife, a public relations expert, had urged me not to appear on the Rightwing show nor to attend the CTD meeting. She wouldn't say, "I told you so," but her look and her silence would speak louder than my ears—or my conscience—could easily tolerate. Feeling too frustrated and furious to open my mail or respond to the blinking phone message light, I opened my bottom desk drawer where I kept a bottle of cognac for special occasions. This was, I decided, a special occasion. As I sipped the liquor, I thought about the Freedom of Employment Act story. Geneva's tales usually brought me praise, not persecution. Here, of course, the hypothetical act had been ripped out of the context of a much longer article. Even so, could I have garbled it in the writing so as to give comfort to our enemies and serious grief to black people generally, including me?

I went to my four-drawer filing cabinet and, after some searching, pulled out the large and unwieldy file of all the stories Geneva had told me or we had worked out together. As I began perusing the pages, I reached, without looking, for my drink. A mistake. I brushed against the glass, shoving it beyond the desk's edge, and then, as I lunged to catch it before it fell, the file tumbled out of my lap, scattering its papers all over the floor. Another sign, as if I needed it, that this was not my day.

Can the Lord be testing my forbearance? I wondered, as I knelt to retrieve the papers. Well, I sure as hell am failing the test. And what's that sheaf labeled "First Draft"? It didn't look like any of the stories in my first two books, but more like a script for a play of some kind. As I paged through it, its origin came back to me. It was the start of what Geneva and I had hoped would make a great film about her car crash in Mississippi, the one that precipitated her years-long coma. She had given me all the details for a drama we hoped would portray the courage of the many long-subordinated people who determined in the early 1960s to be free whatever the cost.

I smiled remembering the hours we spent arguing over who would play her part. "She has to be six feet five and as black as I am, or it will not work!" Geneva had insisted.

"Well," I'd said brightly, "there's Grace Jones, she of the high-fashion clothes that usually reveal ample amounts of her very impressive figure."

Geneva would give me her "Please!" look. "Jones is tall and black enough, but she is not my style. I am a lawyer, after all."

"How about Rosalind Cash or Gloria Foster. They're both dynamic, tall, though not as tall as you, and—"

"And much too light in complexion," Geneva would interrupt. "They will not do. My blackness is who I am."

As I recall, we had settled on Cicely Tyson as dark enough and with acting prowess sufficient to convince anyone that she is ten feet tall. Well, we never reached the casting problem. I had sent our partial draft to a few friends in the film industry, but nothing came of it. Evidently, I'd filed it away and forgotten it. I settled back in my comfortable chair. Maybe the script could recall those exciting times when the danger was real but the mission clear, the soldiers true.

DEEP SOUTH, RURAL TOWN, GAS STATION

It is dusk, the end of a hot summer day. The time is the mid-1960s. A half-dozen or so white, working-class "good ole boys" are grouped around a bench in front of a rundown two-pump gas station. Beside a small office, there is a one-car garage, to the side of which stands a souped-up pickup truck. An outdoor phone is attached to the wall. A faded sign over the station garage reads, Moultree's Oil, Gas, Repairs. The men, dressed in farmer's bib overalls and plaid shirts or in khaki pants and undershirts, are horsing around, drinking beer, and chiding a teenager, BUDDY, who refuses to drink with them. MOUL-TREE, the owner of the gas station an older man, and a figure of authority, points his beer at the boy.

MOULTREE

Come on, Buddy boy! Jus' 'cause you finish high school and hopin' to go to that ragged-ass state college over in Greenville, don' mean you cain't join us with one of these beers.

BUDDY

(Hangs his head, obviously not wanting to argue.) Mr. Moultree, this Coke is jus' fine.

The other Good Ole Boys hoot at the remark. They joke about the benefits of not finishing school and boast about how little schooling each has.

ANDY

(Fat redneck, beer-belly, a troublemaker and proud of it, looks at Moultree.) Guess you ain't tol' him, Moultree. Don' drink wit' the boys, cain't work at Moultree's. And cain't work at Moultree's, cain't afford to go to college."

J. T.

(Tall, relatively slender in comparison with the others. Grimaces to show he doesn't like Andy's comment.) You wrong on both counts, Andy. My baby brother wants to work, but he got one of those whatcha call 'em—schol-arships. An' it ain't at no state college. It's Ole Miss."

BUDDY

(Frowns at his brother: where he hopes to go to college was supposed to stay in the family until everything is worked out.)

The Good Ole Boys are surprised and impressed by the news; they are also envious and even more eager to cut Buddy down to size.

MOULTREE

(In a dominating, almost threatening tone.) You better off at State, boy. Ole Miss ain't Ole Miss no more now the Feds done forced that nigger James Meredith in there. Looks like white men cain't have nothin' to 'emselves no more. Watch what I say, niggers goin' take over the whole damn state.

The Good Ole Boys make faces expressing disgust and declare, cursing, that they are not going to let it happen.

J. T.

(With vehemence, not wanting to be on the wrong side of this issue.) You right there, Clem. Mama 'n' Daddy wranglin' over this thing ever since Buddy got the letter. Daddy say no chile o' his'n goin' to no school that takes in niggers. Mama let him talk, but my money say Buddy goin' to Ole Miss.

TODD

(The eldest of the group, with little hair, fewer teeth, sits on a barrel.) I tell you. Our niggers was happy till them Northern do-gooders come down here stirrin' em' up. My granpappy tol' me same thing happened after the Confederacy. Northern do-gooders swarm in here like flies on horseshit, gave our darkies all manner o' big

ideas. They got tired after while. Left on their own—
though we helped some git on back where they come
from. Then we scared the niggers back into shape.
Happen before, it'll happen again. Mark my word!

ANDY

Damn right, Todd. Way it suppos' to be. White man
take what he want. Niggers get the leftovers. Fair and
square's how I see it.

BUDDY

(*Looks hard at Andy, then at the rest of the group. He
speaks in a low voice, with some feeling.*) Been readin'
a lot and thinkin' a lot. Sure, we whites kin have what
we want long as what we want's drinkin' beer in the
heat and dust 'round a two-pump station out in the
country. That, and keepin' niggers down. None of us
got much of nothin' worthwhile. Meantime, the fat cats
runnin' the companies and gettin' themselves elected
to high office livin' better 'n we ever dream. When we
goin' to get smart?

J. T.

(*Embarrassed at his brother's remarks, which distance
him from the only group he knows.*) We goin' to get
real smart after you finis' college, Buddy. You goin'
smart us up real good. Right, boys?

*The Good Ole Boys laugh long and hard at Buddy's expense.
Buddy lapses back into silence, staring at the Coke bottle in his
hand.*

TODD

(*Looks at Buddy hard. He is serious, not laughing.*)
Naw, J. T. He ain't gonna smart us up. White boys go to
college, get in line for good-payin' jobs, marry them

trophy women with long hair, hands ain't never been in no soapsuds. Buddy go to college, won't have no time for the likes of us. Soon be one of them fat cats, treatin' us like we niggers. He too young to know. We ain't got no choice. Got to treat the darkies bad so they cain't forget they on the bottom—not us.

All eyes turn at the sound of a deep-throated engine. A classic, though far from mint condition, Jaguar roadster pulls up to the outdoor phone. Those eyes harden as GENEVA CRENSHAW, *a very tall black woman, emerges from the car. She is striking in a two-piece, white linen suit, one suitable for a courtroom; even in the heat of the early evening, she exudes a cool elegance. Ignoring the hostile stares of the white men, she walks quickly to the phone, deposits several coins, and dials.*

SANCTUARY OF SMALL RURAL BLACK CHURCH

The REVEREND BARNES, *a large black man with a clerical collar, is leading twenty-five or so black men and women who, their voices fervent but ragged, are singing a hymn. In an office off to the side, a telephone rings—and rings. Finally the Reverend Barnes gestures to the group to continue singing and goes to answer the phone. He is frowning in worry as he picks up the receiver. He places his other hand over his ear to hear over the singing, and, in a wary tone, answers.*

REV. BARNES
Hello. Reverend Barnes here. *(Recognizing the caller, he is relieved, though still anxious.)* Thank God, Lawyer Crenshaw! You O.K.? We been gettin' a mite worried. I hope you're still comin' to our meetin'. With folks bein' fired, havin' their loans canceled and all, we need the kind of reassurance only you can bring us.

GAS STATION

All the men are still staring as Geneva speaks on the phone.

MOULTREE
(Both sneering and taunting, his Southern drawl exaggerated.) Boys, what you gawkin' at couldn't be seen in my day. Any blacks dare let the sun set on 'em in this town not be alive next mornin'. My daddy didn't let 'em light on this station 'ceptin' to clean up. He likely turnin' in his grave to see good white men standin' by while this uppity black bitch from up North showin' off her damned fancy car roun' down hyar stirring' up our niggers.

GENEVA
(Returns cold stare of white men staring at her.) Don't worry, Reverend Barnes. The court case back in Jackson lasted all day, but I am on my way. Tell your people I'll be there in thirty minutes. *(Listens as Barnes speaks.)* No, Attorney Bell was not able to come with me. I'm alone, but after two years down here, I know my way around the Delta. Any of these rednecks try to cause me trouble, my car is fast enough to get me out of it. *(Geneva hangs up the phone, walks swiftly back to her car, gets in, and drives away from the station.)*

TWO-LANE HIGHWAY

It is getting dark enough for headlights, and the camera follows the Jaguar's rear lights as Geneva speeds down a road cutting, arrow-straight, through cotton fields on both sides. A cloud of dust rises in her wake.

GAS STATION

The rednecks stare after the car, cursing.

MOULTREE

(His tone even more provocative.) Hey, J. T., you done spent the whole damn summer fittin' that big Chrysler engine in that half-ass pickup of yourn. Les' give that nigger bitch a lil' scare. I got a ten-dollar bill say you cain't catch that fancy-ass, furrin sports car o' hers!

J. T.

(Eagerly accepting challenge.) Get your damn money ready, Moultree! I can catch her. Come on Buddy! You my witness.

Buddy hangs back, but J. T. grabs him by the arm and pulls him toward the pickup truck parked beside the station garage. The truck looks powerful, with raised suspension, oversize tires, spotlights mounted above the cab; a rifle is suspended above the bench seat. J. T. shoves Buddy into the passenger seat and sprints around to the other side. When J. T. turns the ignition switch, the engine roars to life. He shifts into gear, spins his wheels creating a shower of gravel, and charges off.

HIGHWAY CHASE

As J. T. starts down the two-lane highway after Geneva, he can hardly see the Jaguar's tail lights. Even so, his souped-up truck begins to close the distance between them.

Spotting the pickup's four headlights in her rearview mirror, Geneva senses danger and increases her speed. The speedometer moves up to 90, then to 95. Even so, the truck's lights are larger, closer. Realizing that she can't outrun the truck, she

*slows somewhat and allows it to come within 150 feet. Then
she hits the brakes and, whipping the steering wheel hard to
the left, does a 180-degree spin to speed back past the truck
heading in the opposite direction.*

J. T.
(*In the pickup, muttering curses.*) Bitch must think she
haulin' moonshine. Buddy, let's show her we do haul
moonshine.

*Buddy, his eyes wide with fear, does not respond. J. T. executes
the same 180-degree skid turn and, again, gives chase.*

GENEVA
(*Watching the pickup lights close in behind her, bites
her lip in concentration and speaks coolly to herself.*)
Geneva, chile, you are going the wrong way to reach
Reverend Barnes's church, and those rednecks are
gaining on you. It is time to poop or get off the pot!

*Hitting her brakes, Geneva again spins her car in the opposite
direction. She pushes hard on the accelerator, but this time
swerves into the middle of the two-lane road, and shoots
toward the truck, straddling the white line.*

J. T.
(*Seeing Geneva's car heading toward him, recognizes
immediately that she is challenging him. "Chicken" is
just his kind of game. He pushes the gas pedal to the
floor.*) My pickup'll squash that crazy black bitch like a
bug!

BUDDY
(*Terrified.*) No, no, J. T.!

*At the last instant, he reaches over and yanks the steering wheel
to the right. Although his maneuver avoids a head-on crash, the
truck sideswipes the Jaguar. The car veers off the road and falls,
turning over and over, down the steep bank of a levee. At the
same time, the pickup has careened off the road in the other
direction. It plows into a tree and explodes in a ball of flames.*

Reading that script again, recalling Geneva's courage, with-
ered my anger and humbled me. I realized that I was acting as
mindless as those rednecks, taking out my anger against the
CTD members while forgetting the real culprits, the reac-
tionary congresspeople who were making political hay with my
satire. Here I was worrying about my reputation while so many
were putting their lives on the line for the cause. Geneva had
been one of those whose courage served as an inspiration. Back
then, when she aimed her Jaguar down the center of that country road, and pushed the gas pedal to the floorboard, she was
challenging not only the big pickup that had been harassing
her, but also the systematic intimidation of blacks that was a
key component of white dominance. Her action—risky, even
suicidal—conveyed a powerful message to whites accustomed
to deferral by blacks: "Whatever the costs, we won't take it any
more."

At that time, Geneva knew—as she and I intended to portray—that those black folks waiting at that church had taken
some very large risks in a state long noted for its willingness to
use violence—and quickly, too—in order to preserve its way of
racial life. The dangers they faced were not unlike those that
cost the lives of the many who dared challenge Mississippi's
racial codes: Medgar Evers, killed in 1963, by a sniper in Jackson; Vernon Dahmer, killed by a firebomb attack in Hattiesburg
in 1966; the New Yorkers Michael Schwerner and Andrew
Goodman, and the Mississippian James E. Chaney, all three
murdered in Neshoba County in 1964.

Geneva could not encourage the people she represented if she personally compromised or exhibited cowardice in the face of intimidation no worse than what they faced daily as they sought what she had assured them was their right to vote, their right to send their children to desegregated schools, their right to live and die in one of the united states of America without being afraid of white people every day of their lives. She simply was not going to allow the whites to intimidate her. Perhaps it is the moral strength gained through commitment at this level that in Geneva's case—and likely that of many others—enabled the making of a way out of no way.

What if all black folks adopted Geneva's attitude? I wondered. What if they, too, were to refuse to "take low" when whites demand subordination—or else? Would racism end, and quite quickly? Or, would we all be killed—also quite quickly?

8

NIGGER FREE

We have come over a way that with tears has been
*   watered,*
We have come, treading our path thro' the blood of
*   the slaughtered,*
Out from the gloomy past, till now we stand at last
Where the white gleam of our bright star is cast.
—James Weldon Johnson and J. Rosamond Johnson

Late as it was, I still had to read the four student papers I'd been carrying around in my briefcase. I read through and made notes on three of them. Weary and yawning, I turned to the last paper, determined to finish it before heading home. Its title— "Riots: America's Synonym for Racial Massacres"—was promising. Two students had labored on this paper for most of the school year and hoped to get it published in a law review. They had gotten the idea for it after a heated argument in my civil rights class on whether the slaughter of uncounted hundreds of blacks during America's many race riots were a form of genocide.

The few white students who were aware of these riot-massacres maintained that, however horrific, they did not constitute genocide as they were defining it: that is, "a coordinated plan of different actions aiming at the destruction of essential foundations of the life of national groups, with the aim of annihilating the groups themselves." Such genocide was, in the first half of the twentieth century, the Holocaust in Nazi Germany and, in the second, the government-ordered murder of millions in Cambodia, Africa, India, Bosnia, and elsewhere around the world. My class had no trouble agreeing that the utter decimation of Native Americans in this country and of the so-called aborigines in Australia was often a result of unacknowledged government policy.

Several black students argued vigorously that the government's nonresponse or inadequate response—when mobs of whites rampaged through black communities, burning houses and killing every black person they could find—was so usual as to be predictable and relied on by the rampaging whites, and thus constituted genocide. In support of this position of government complicity, the paper's authors had found and analyzed patterns of atrocity motivated by a determination not simply to kill blacks—often in indescribably horrible ways—but to remove them from the community, either economically (by destruction of their property and refusing them employment) or emotionally (through spirit-deadening intimidation).

My students have done their research well, I thought as I read. In addressing the white students' assertion that genocide, as they defined it, could never happen in modern-day America, these black students presented in graphic detail what had happened in the past so as to demonstrate the emptiness of any such benign assurances about the present. Here they quoted James Baldwin's reaction to the Holocaust and his empathy for the Jews:

> I could not but feel, in those sorrowful years, that this human indifference, concerning which I knew so much already, would be my portion on the day that the United States decided to murder Negroes systematically instead

of little by little and catch-as-catch can. I was, of course, authoritatively assured that what had happened to the Jews in Germany could not happen to the Negroes in America, but I thought, bleakly, that the German Jews had probably believed similar counselors.

The Mormon experience indicates that, once the killing begins, the government may find political reasons not to intervene. Throughout the mid-1800s, members of the Church of Latter-Day Saints (Mormons) were persecuted by violent mobs from New York to Missouri. Church members were tarred and feathered, driven from their homes and property, imprisoned, and murdered. These persecutions escalated to state-mandated genocide in 1838, when Governor Lillburn W. Boggs of Missouri ordered: "The Mormons must be treated as enemies and *must be exterminated.*" In November 1839, church representatives petitioned President Martin Van Buren for assistance. After hearing of the atrocities, President Van Buren responded: "Gentlemen, your cause is just, but I can do nothing for you. . . . If I take up for you, I shall lose the vote of Missouri."

Reading about those past riot-massacres was, while enthralling, also deeply unsettling. Somewhere in midmanuscript, two words flashed before my eyes: **Nigger Free.** I blinked. The words disappeared. But, again, a few pages later, **Nigger Free** flashed and, again, disappeared. Has Geneva returned, I wondered, with another of her little tricks? I looked around the office.

"Geneva," I called, "cut it out!" No response. But, of course, she was still on a cross-country mission, which she has been secretive about. Moreover, she hates the "*n* word," as she calls it.

Sighing, I returned to my students' paper, more and more involved with those multitudes of black people whose worst nightmares about life in a racist society had proven fatally accurate. Absorbed in the horrors of the past, I gradually got used to that intermittent flash of **Nigger Free.**

Philadelphia, Pennsylvania (1834). In midsummer, from four hundred to five hundred whites, incensed by the hiring of Negroes while whites were unemployed, invaded the Flying Horse, an amusement area in the city's black section, attempting to drive the Negroes out. In the street fight that ensued, the blacks repulsed white attackers. In retaliation, the following night, a large mob of whites rampaged through black neighborhoods, destroying thirty-one homes and two churches and beating blacks. One black, Stephen James, was killed. The town meeting condemned the riots and voted reimbursements for the damage, but criticized the blacks for harboring fugitive slaves and making noise in their churches. Blacks were urged to behave "inoffensively" and not be "obtrusive" in passing along the streets or in assembling together. The Philadelphia riots sparked similar outbreaks in Columbia, Pennsylvania; in Trenton, Southwark, Lancaster, and Bloomfield, New Jersey; and in Rochester, New York, and New York City. Throughout the antebellum years, attacks on blacks and their property were a favorite sport of the white working class.

Nigger Free

New York City (1863). In March 1863, halfway into the Civil War, the federal government found itself unable to raise enough troops for the Union Army, and enacted a conscription act to which only white males were subject. Draftees, selected by a lottery, could avoid service by presenting an "acceptable substitute" or paying three hundred dollars, an exemption beyond the means of working-class whites. Race relations in the city were already tense with continuing threats and occasional assaults on black working men; the situation was exacerbated when shipping companies began employing black labor to break a longshoremen's strike. On 13 July, the first day of the draft lottery, hundreds of white workers stayed away from their jobs, marched through the city, and began five days of rioting.

They burned down the federal building where the draft lottery was held, and destroyed other symbols of federal authority. Blacks, though, were the major victims of their wrath. Whites set afire the Colored Orphan Asylum in New York. They roamed the city streets setting upon, beating, and killing dozens of blacks. In lower Manhattan, dockworkers, who had for years prohibited blacks from working on the wharves, now determined to drive away any blacks who lived in the area. Tenements housing black families were torched, and the victims' furniture was demolished and burned in sidewalk bonfires. George Spriggs, a black laborer, was evicted by his white landlord, who feared that, if Spriggs remained, the mob would burn down the house.

A black shoemaker, James Costello, was chased by a young white man on West Thirty-second Street. He fired a shot, but his effort at self-defense served to draw the attention of five or six white laborers. After pulling Costello from the house where he had sought refuge, they beat, kicked, and stoned him, trampled on his body, and finally hanged him. Half dead, he was dragged to a mudhole and immersed in water while the mob emptied a barrel of ashes over his head. The mob then plundered and burned down the house where Costello had tried to hide. Black men were the major targets of mob fury, but black women who tried to protect their husbands and sons were also attacked. After a few days, the rioters had emptied the harbor front of people of color. Black families sought refuge in Central Park or across the river in New Jersey. One eyewitness reported acts of horrendous cruelty inflicted on the city's black population:

A child of 3 years of age was thrown from a 4th story window and instantly killed. A woman one hour after her confinement was set upon and beaten with her tender babe in her arms. . . . Children were torn from their mother's embrace and their brains blown out in the very face of the afflicted mother. Men were burnt by slow fires.

Nigger Free

Memphis, Tennessee (1866). A failed attempt by police to halt alleged disorderly conduct by black soldiers prompted whites to begin a general massacre. During it, forty-six blacks and two whites were killed, about seventy-five were wounded, and ninety homes, twelve schools, and four black churches were burned. E. L. Godkin, co-founder of *The Nation* and its editor at the time, wrote that the killing was "inconceivably brutal, but . . . [i]ts most novel and most striking incident was that the *police* headed the butchery, and roved round the town either in company with the white mob or singly, and occupied themselves in shooting down every colored person, of whatever sex, of whom they got a glimpse."

Nigger Free

Colfax, Louisiana (1872). In the wake of the gubernatorial election of 1872, both the Republican and the Democratic parties claimed victory. Republicans, fearing that the Democrats— Southern whites absolutely opposed to their former slaves gaining the attributes of citizenship—might try to seize the government, urged blacks to cordon off the county seat in Grant Parish and to set up defenses. The blacks held the tiny town for three weeks, but were overpowered by whites armed with rifles and a small cannon. An indiscriminate slaughter followed, including the massacre of some fifty blacks who laid down their arms under a white flag of surrender. Two hundred and eighty blacks were killed. Two whites also died. The state government took no action; and while the Justice Department indicted ninety-six persons for violating federal civil rights laws, only nine were found guilty—not of murder, but of violating the blacks' civil rights. Four years later, the Supreme Court, applying the narrowest interpretation of the civil rights laws, overturned these convictions.

Nigger Free

Atlanta, Georgia (1906). The largest riot in the Deep South between 1900 and 1910 began on 24 September 1906 and followed the usual pattern: racial tensions heightened by politicians seeking to disenfranchise blacks, and an irresponsible press offering a reward for a "lynching bee." Black people began arming themselves; and the police, while arresting blacks for being armed, shot into a crowd. In the return fire, one officer was killed and another injured. Whites then began a general destruction of Negro property and lives. In the ensuing violence, at least four blacks who were substantial citizens were killed and many injured. Negro homes were looted and burned. For several days, the city was paralyzed: factories were closed, and all transportation stopped. Numerous blacks sold their property and left the area.

Nigger Free

East St. Louis Riots (1917). Between 1915 and 1919, there were some eighteen major interracial disturbances across the country. In July 1917, serious racial violence occurred in Chester and Philadelphia, Pennsylvania, and in Houston, Texas. In East St. Louis, Missouri, at least thirty-nine blacks and nine whites were killed in riots. Six thousand blacks were driven from their homes. President Woodrow Wilson's secretary told the press that the details of the riot were so sickening that he found it difficult to read about them; the President himself took no action and, despite press criticism, remained silent.

Wilson, like most of America's presidents, was reluctant even to speak out on lynching and other racial violence.

Congress did appoint an investigative committee, which reported that racial tensions had been brought to the boiling point by the mills, factories, and railroads that were importing ten thousand to twelve thousand blacks from the Deep South with the promise of good jobs. In fact, these companies wanted a pool of cheap black labor to counteract the labor unions' efforts to organize white workers. Many of the blacks who came north found neither work nor decent places to live. They crowded into East St. Louis, swelling its already large black population; and the town became a center of lawlessness.

The rioting began on 2 July, when an unidentified car drove through the colored section firing indiscriminately into homes. Armed blacks, alerted by a prearranged signal (the ringing of a church bell), flocked into the streets and attacked a police car that had come to investigate the disturbance. The crowd fired volleys of shots into the car, killing two officers. The next day, mobs of blacks killed other whites. Whites, learning of these attacks, began to retaliate by attacking every black person in sight.

A black man, "trying to escape from a mob of thirty or forty men, was knocked down, kicked in the face, beaten into insensibility; and then a man stood over him and shot him five times as he lay helpless in the street."

The congressional committee also reported:

> All fared alike, young and old, women and children; none was spared. The crowd soon grew to riotous proportions, and for hours the manhunt continued, stabbing, clubbing, and shooting, not the guilty but unoffending negroes. One was hanged from a telephone pole, and another had a rope tied around his neck and was dragged through the

streets, the maddened crowd kicking him and beating him as he lay prostrate and helpless.

The negroes were pursued into their homes, and the torch completed the work of destruction. As they fled from the flames they were shot down, although many of them came out with uplifted hands, pleading to be spared.

It was a day and night given over to arson and murder. Scenes of horror that would have shocked a savage were viewed with placid unconcern by hundreds whose hearts knew no pity, and who seemed to revel in the feast of blood and cruelty.

It is not possible to give accurately the number of dead. At least thirty-nine negroes and eight white people were killed outright, and hundreds of negroes were wounded and maimed. "The bodies of the dead negroes," testified an eyewitness, "were thrown into a morgue like so many dead hogs."

The committee reported that police failed to halt the violence and often participated in it. When soldiers of the state militia took rioters to jail, the police released them by the hundreds without bond and without making any effort to identify them. When the mob held several policemen against a wall while other rioters were assaulting blacks, the police made no effort to free themselves, deeming the situation highly humorous. At one point, the committee reports: "The police shot into a crowd of negroes who were huddled together, making no resistance. It was a particularly cowardly exhibition of savagery." The report indicates that many of the soldiers joined the rioters, later boasting of how many blacks they had killed.

Nigger Free

Chicago Riots (1919). Considering how bloody it was, James Weldon Johnson called the summer of 1919 the "Red Summer." From June to the end of that year, there were approximately twenty-five race riots. As many blacks came to Chicago as to East St. Louis seeking work and competing for jobs with white laborers. The riots climaxed a series of increasingly serious racial clashes. A provocation for the Chicago riots of 1919 had occurred a few weeks before, when two black men were killed on their way home from work. Joseph Robinson, a laborer, was attacked by a gang of white toughs and stabbed to death. Sanford Harris passed a group of whites. When they threatened him, he ran, but was shot to death by one of the gang. Policemen who came on the scene made no arrests even though a white woman pointed out the assailant.

Blacks and whites armed themselves, while city officials did nothing, hoping that somehow the anger on each side would subside. Of course, it did not. The incident that sparked the Chicago riot was the drowning of a black youth whom whites had stoned after he ventured across an imaginary line in the water of Lake Michigan separating the black and white beaches. There followed several days of attacks on blacks going to and from work, or walking the streets, particularly in "white" areas. Blacks fought back, and several whites were killed or injured. Blacks living among white neighbors in Englewood, far to the south, were driven from their homes, their household goods were stolen, and their houses were burned or wrecked. Police proved generally ineffective in halting the violence, and reports indicated that some of the police actually participated in the rioting as well as neglected their duty. During the height of the rioting, 2,800 of the 3,000-man police force were assigned to the "Black Belt," but there were few police in the areas where most of the injuries occurred. The total casualties were 38 deaths—15 white, 23 black—and 537 people injured.

Nigger Free

Elaine, Arkansas (1919). The First World War was followed by a period of political and economic change similar to that after the Civil War. Both wars ended in victories that offered hope to blacks that they would at last gain the freedom to enter the marketplace and compete with whites rather than be exploited by them. In October 1919, black sharecroppers in Elaine, Arkansas, campaigned for a fair share of the prices their crops brought in the market; as a result, they were attacked by whites, and both whites and blacks died. State troops, called in to quell the disturbances, joined with the whites and rounded up the blacks and placed them in a stockade. The white troops refused to allow the captive blacks any contact with family or attorneys, and would release them only if a white person vouched for them; for many blacks, this support was forthcoming only if they agreed to work for the white patron for a period at wages set by the latter. During the fighting, at least five whites were killed. A month later, after hasty trials for murder in which the black defenders were not permitted to call witnesses, twelve blacks were sentenced to death and subsequently executed. Twelve other blacks were convicted of second-degree murder; they were sentenced to twenty-one years in the state penitentiary.

Nigger Free

Tulsa Riots (1921). As a result of an oil boom, Tulsa was a crime-racked, corruption-ridden Oklahoma town, where no one had much respect for law. In May 1921, Tulsa's blacks feared that a young black man charged with molesting a white female elevator operator—he had accidentally stepped on her toe—might be lynched (as a white man accused of murder had been a few months earlier). Twenty-five armed blacks marched to the jail and offered to help the sheriff protect the youth. Despite the sheriff's insistence that no harm would come to the black man, rumors of a lynching persisted, and seventy-five armed blacks returned to the jail. A scuffle with whites resulted, shooting started, and two blacks and ten whites were killed. When the outnumbered blacks retreated to the black community, whites looted hardware and sporting-goods stores, arming themselves with rifles, revolvers, and ammunition. Large groups of whites and blacks fired on each other. Whites then decided to invade "Niggertown" and systematically wipe it out.

To accomplish this end, more than ten thousand armed whites massed for the invasion, sixty to eighty automobiles filled with armed whites formed a circle around the black section, while airplanes were used to spy on the movements of blacks and—according to some reports—drop bombs on them. Black men and women fought valiantly but vainly to defend their homes against the hordes of invaders who, after looting the homes, set them on fire. Blacks seeking to escape the flames were shot down.

> The heaviest fighting occurred in the northern section, where hundreds of blacks concentrated in a valley. Fifty or more barricaded themselves in a church. The whites launched several massed attacks against the church, but each time the attackers fell back under fire from the black defenders. Finally, a torch applied to the church set it ablaze, and the occupants began to pour out, shooting as they ran. Several blacks were killed. . . .
>
> The entire black belt became a smoldering heap of blackened ruins. Hardly a shanty, house, or building was left standing throughout the area. Domestic animals wandering among the wreckage gave the only signs of life in the desolated territory.

Thousands of blacks, unable to get far from the scene, camped on hills surrounding the city. They were aided by the Red Cross and local social agencies. Unofficial estimates put the death toll at 50 whites and from 150 to 200 blacks, many of whom were buried in graves without coffins. Other victims, incinerated in the burning houses, were never accounted for.

Nigger Free

The Rosewood Massacre (1923). Rosewood, Florida, was a black community of about twenty families. Many owned their own homes as well as other property. There was a one-room school, at least two churches, and a Masonic lodge. In response to a white woman's allegation that she had been attacked by an unidentified black man, a group of white men killed one black man and, a few days later, attacked the large, nine-bedroom home of the Carriers, a black family in Rosewood, where the family and several friends decided to defend themselves. In the gun battle, Sarah and Sylvester Carrier were killed, and other family members were wounded. Two white men were killed, and several wounded. One black man was shot to death on the graves of his mother and brother when he refused to tell his white captors the names of those who had fired on the white men.

When the whites left to get more ammunition, Rosewood's residents fled into the surrounding swamps; there they were hunted like animals through the thickets by hundreds of white men who returned to Rosewood and burned down every structure in the town. Newspaper accounts of the time described the scene as a race riot with lynching, shootings, mass graves, mutilations, and burnings. A recent account reports:

> People came from all around to take part in the manhunt. They were people with a thirst for blood. The remaining survivors of Rosewood . . . are still tortured with the lingering image of a parent or grandparent being lynched or shot, of the family home being burned to the ground, of crawling through the woods in the dead of night and hiding from an armed and crazy mob; of being hunted and attacked for nothing more than their color.

Finally, survivors were evacuated by train and taken to Gainesville. Subsequently, a grand jury was convened to investigate, but it returned no indictments. In 1994, the Florida legislature passed, and the governor signed, a controversial claim bill providing $60,000 in scholarships to compensate the Rosewood families and their survivors.

Nigger Free

Equally grim were my students' reports of later riots: New York City in 1935, Detroit in 1943, Los Angeles in 1965. And equally predictable were the patterns of cause, casualties, and subsequent investigating committees. Whether a race riot had been sparked by black or white violence, it always resulted in blacks suffering a disproportionate number of deaths, injuries, and loss of property. And once the fighting began, law-enforcement forces could not be relied on for protection and often gave aid and support to white rioters.

Riots were, my students contended, but the most dramatic, active components of the unacknowledged desire of many whites to rid America of black people. The lynchings that often occurred during a riot were usually carried out by relatively small groups, sometimes organized by the Klan, more often the impulsive actions of an enraged few. Lynchings took the lives of at least five thousand blacks in the years between 1859 and 1969. Few, if any, of the perpetrators were ever brought to justice. According to a scholar of the period, lynchers had "little to fear from those who administered the southern legal system," and prosecutors often dismissed lynchings as "an expression of the will of the people." In the year 1900, for example, there were 105 reported lynchings; and white mobs assaulted blacks in New Orleans for three days, burning and robbing their homes and stores. Such violence did not prevent the first of several antilynching measures—this one introduced by G. H. White, a black congressman from North Carolina—from dying in committee. Despite earnest campaigns by the NAACP and other groups, the Congress never passed any of the antilynching bills placed before it.

It is simply impossible, my students argue, to estimate the number of blacks murdered by individual whites whose motive was sheer racial antagonism. Only a small number of those who commit these crimes are tried for them. Few are convicted. These killings continue. On the other hand, when blacks, also motivated primarily by racial hate, kill whites, the response by law-enforcement agencies and the public is swift and often deadly.

My students predict that the economic motivation behind racial hatred and racial violence will be as strong in the future as in the past. To support this view, they cite Dionne Brand, the black Canadian feminist, who writes, of America as well as Canada, that "North America does not need Black people anymore . . . for the cheap and degraded labor we've represented across the centuries of our lives here." And Brand asks, "Why empower a Black person in America to demand better wages and better working conditions," when you can ship the work off to an unenfranchised Colombian or Sri Lankan who is willing to work for pennies in miserably inadequate and unsanitary conditions?

Nigger Free

I blinked at the flashing words, no less disconcerting even as my eyes were closing in fatigue. I pushed on to the paper's conclusion. Because of our perceived obsolescence as a source of labor, and our vulnerability as scapegoats in economically bad times, black Americans are more at risk of genocidal policies than ever before. My students suggest an additional component of this danger. Despite America's history of race riots, lynchings, and homicides, violent revolution—the ultimate response of oppressed people to their oppression—is not available to African Americans. James Weldon Johnson's conclusion in the 1930s that a violent response to racial injustice is justified, but futile, is no less accurate today. Black people simply lack the numbers and the resources to mount an armed revolt. This realization, while providing a pragmatic component to the philosophical doctrine of nonviolent protest, also serves to redirect black rage from the perpetrators of racist policies and practices to other blacks who become victims of violence for which whites can claim they are not responsible. Calling the phenomenon "intra-inflicted genocide," my students argue that, if less dramatic, it is no less a devastating form of government-sponsored genocide.

Nigger Free

I rubbed my eyes again; then sat back and closed them. All those heartrending accounts of mayhem inflicted by one set of human beings on another were jumbling together in my mind, getting to me, making me feel odd and disoriented. Suddenly I heard the roar of a large crowd, alternately cheering and jeering, as though they were watching a sporting event. Interspersed with the discord was the crash of broken glass and what sounded like firecrackers—or gunfire. The crowd seemed blocks away, but coming closer, getting louder. It was scary. What was going on?

I opened my eyes, got up, and turned off the lights. I looked out the window onto Washington Square Park. There was a red glow in the night sky, and the air was acrid with the smoke from dozens of fires. Looking to the west, I could see a raucous mob coming toward me, running down Fourth Street toward the park. They were shattering every window they passed, overturning cars, brandishing guns and shooting at random. I had never seen anything like it. And I didn't have to guess at the mob's intentions.

With a bloodcurdling cheer, several rioters in the park discovered a black man with his white girlfriend trying to hide behind a hedge. I saw the couple running south toward the law school, no doubt seeking refuge there. I couldn't see the front gates, but the yelling, the shots fired, the horrible triumphal cheering "We got the nigger and the nigger-loving bitch!" told me those gates had already been locked.

Before I could digest the young couple's likely fate, I heard a quick knock on my door and a voice. "Professor, are you there?"

I recognized the security guard's voice, pulled down the window shades, put on a desk lamp, then opened the door. "It's good to see you, Sergeant Casey, but where in hell are the police?"

"Not sure, sir. We've been calling them. That mob is movin' on for the moment, but they or another like them will be back, and those gates won't hold them next time. I'm supposed to evacuate the building."

I looked at him in astonishment. "You've got to be joking. You may be safe out there, but as a black man, my life won't be worth anything. I'll take my chances right here in my office."

"I'm sorry, Professor, this thing is very, very bad. The TV reports are awful. My orders are to get you out of here at once, sir," he said. "The only thing that may stop the mob tonight," he went on, "is one of the signs we're posting now on every building in the university stating there are no black people inside."

"What kind of sign?" I asked, feeling I already knew.

The sergeant reached into a large manila folder he was carrying, and pulled out a sheet of cardboard. Yes, there it was: **Nigger Free.**

"I'm sorry sir. We'll take them down tomorrow. We expect federal troops will arrive and end this thing. But we have to get through the night. You understand, sir."

I did understand. "Great for the buildings, Sergeant Casey. But you must have dozens, hundreds actually, of black and dark-skinned Hispanic students, faculty, administrators, workers around the campus. What about them?"

"We're organizing a fleet of armed buses to take everyone who needs refuge to a place in New Jersey where they'll be safe until this thing ends."

"Very thoughtful, Sergeant." I tried and failed to imagine what kind of armor short of Sherman tanks could protect blacks against that mob. "Well, post your damn signs if you must, but I am not leaving this office!"

The sergeant looked perplexed, then nodded. "I understand, Professor. I could force you out, but I've known you for five, six years. You always speak or stop to share a few words. Not just me, all the guards, and the mail people, the copy-room guys, even the janitors. Thing is, though, unless you leave, I could lose my job. And if, somehow, the mob finds you here, they'll trash the building, and there'll be no more law school— or not for a long time. But it's up to you, sir, your decision."

"Right! Really great options you give me, Sergeant." I started to pack my briefcase, then left it on my desk, and put a few computer diskettes containing important files in my pocket. I turned to the sergeant. "I'm ready." He nodded and led me toward the back stairs of the now darkened building.

We reached a side entrance just as the first of two large buses pulled up on MacDougal Street, flanked by four or five NYU security cars, each with a driver and two security persons with rifles. As I stepped up to board the bus, I could hear the mob's roar. They must be heading back our way. Pausing, I looked in the bus and saw it full of frightened faces. Then I looked down Fourth Street and saw, perhaps a block away, four young white toughs and, behind them, the yelling mob. I knew that the buses and their occupants would not stand a chance against that flood of angry people.

"Hey, you S.O.B.'s!" I yelled.

I jumped off the bus steps and dashed toward the four

hoodlums. As they started toward me, screaming threats, I turned, heading back along Fourth Street, away from the buses.

Ignoring them, the hoodlums sprinted after me. In my brief glimpse of them, they'd looked to be about twenty, a third my age, but they also looked as though they'd been drinking, and I hoped they didn't do anything like my daily three-mile run. I loped along, thankful that I was wearing my running shoes and old khaki slacks. I was less happy about my Rainbow Coalition sweatshirt with Jesse Jackson's picture emblazoned on the front. Still, I thought, if those guys catch me, not even a Rush Limbaugh shirt would save me. The men were within thirty yards now, and I sprinted for about two hundred yards, hoping to discourage them.

They kept coming, but even easing back to a more comfortable pace, one I hoped I could maintain for two miles, I began to pull away from three of them. The fourth was gaining on me. I was moving much faster than my daily pace and could feel the effort in my chest and in my legs. I also felt panic. I couldn't maintain this speed for long. I tried to keep my head. Either keep it, or lose it.

As the tough closed to within about twenty paces, I noticed a large paving brick by the curb. I stopped abruptly, turned, put my hands up in the air. "I give up!" I gasped. My pursuer, breathing hard himself, eased up, certain he had his prey. He was all but upon me, when I quickly, in one motion, bent down, picked up the brick, and smashed it hard in his face. He went down without a sound, his face a mass of blood. I dropped the brick and began to run again, adrenaline fueling me now. I wiped my brow and then my shirt. Both were bloody—his blood, I hoped. I kept running.

I circled back east, then north up Fourth Avenue. My first goal was to reach Central Park at Fifty-ninth Street, some fifty blocks away and halfway home. Heavy black palls of smoke hung in the air, and the deserted streets were strewn with broken glass, other debris, and the bodies of black people. Except for the sound of far-off sirens, there was an eerie silence in this area the rioters had already swept through. I thought of my two grown sons who live in Manhattan, and prayed they were safe. Stores were closed and shuttered, apartment building doors were shut and locked. Jogging along, I listened hard for sounds of mob action and altered my route to avoid it. I was doing this without thinking, on a kind of panic autopilot. The fear that kept me going was accentuated every few seconds by the message on signs—hand-written, printed, even crudely spray-painted on building walls: **Nigger Free.**

That terse message had a painfully ironic ambiguity. Far from using an epithet to announce that blacks were free, it was, as the sergeant had said, telling angry mobs of whites roving the middle-class urban areas and suburbs of New York City that they need not invade any structure or area bearing the sign **Nigger Free.** The apartment buildings, the brownstones, the duplexes, and single-family homes contained no black people. All were gone—or, more accurately, they had been driven out, and along with them whites, Latinos, or Asians who were unfortunate enough to look black or, worse, were thought to be harboring or otherwise trying to protect blacks.

For the dwellers in those buildings, **Nigger Free** insulated them against attack. The sign was a perverse reversal of the "Soul Brother" emblem of the 1960s riots, when blacks rampaged through their neighborhoods sparing, on occasion, those shops where signs denoted black ownership. That night, **Nigger Free** told me, and all the other blacks out on those streets, that there was no refuge behind any door where that sign was posted.

It was a frightening symbol of whites' historic willingness to sacrifice black interests, rights, even our lives, to protect and advance themselves. Symbols, even potent ones, were not, however, my immediate danger. Although I was managing to keep away from the large groups of rioters, it was more difficult to avoid the smaller groups, many of whom were armed. As I ran, I darted into doorways, down side streets I hoped were deserted. Out of breath, I would hide wherever I could, breathe deep for a minute, then begin running again. I was resigned to the worst. The fear that kept me going was less whether I would die, but how. Vivid in my mind were the murders described in my students' paper. As when jogging I try to focus on something other than running, I was now able to put together the background of this "white rage riot" in all its grim detail.

"Racial tensions" was the official characterization of the white hostility that had been increasing with the rise in unemployment and the disappearance of decent jobs across the country, especially in the New York area. For years, many whites believed affirmative action was the culprit, but now all such policies—always more token than substantive—had been eliminated. Fair employment laws, though still on the books, were neither complied with by employers nor enforced by government. Indeed, outright discrimination against blacks in the workforce was, as it had been in the pre-*Brown* era, the order of the day. Even so, as the number of jobless whites continued to mount, so did their irrational rage against black people— many more of whom were jobless.

In the weeks before the "white rage" riots began, there had been a series of "incidents" in which whites and blacks were attacked and injured; a few were killed for no other reason than they belonged to—or, given the nation's nebulous measures of racial identification, seemed to be, might be—the opposite race. Where city officials played down these attacks as individual incidents with no racial significance, the media, more interested in selling advertising than in maintaining calm, hyped up each one. Most vociferous in this effort were two of the nation's most popular talk-show hosts, hatemongers who for years had filled the airwaves with vicious anti-black charges and lies worse even than those two infamous southern senators of the 1930s and 1940s, Theodore Bilbo of Mississippi and Herman Talmadge of Georgia. By now in New York City, white people's fears and frustrations, seesawing daily between government denial and media hype, had reached the breakpoint.

At some point in the last day or so, those feelings had been ignited into violence by the rumor that black teenagers had gunned down those two talk-show hosts in a botched robbery effort outside a midtown nightclub. What had actually happened was that the two men had gotten into a drunken argument inside the club; that it had escalated into a brawl outside, involving each man's coterie of staff, bodyguards, and fans; that shots were fired; and that, finally, several people were wounded and the two talk-show hosts killed. These were the only fatalities. Later, witnesses reported seeing no blacks at all in the area. Even so, for many whites, it was the last straw. It was past time. The niggers had to pay for this atrocity, and they would. **Nigger Free** was watchword, banner, aim.

Within a short time after the false rumors about the killing of the two talk-show hosts, hundreds of small bands of mostly young white men began roaming the streets looking for black people. Because so many black teenagers were armed, they attacked older blacks, women, and children, beating them with bicycle chains and baseball bats, sometimes shooting them. The police did little to stop them. By day's end, larger groups were more systematically searching for blacks. "We're declaring war," they shouted, "on black crime."

Avoiding the police was as important as staying away from these self-appointed black-crime fighters. What I sensed, proved true. The police, when they responded to frantic calls for help, were far more ready to arrest blacks on any excuse than curb the blatant violence of whites. As in earlier riots, units often stood by as blacks were run down and killed. Some policemen actually joined in the killing, able at last to do openly what many had used to do in squad cars and holding rooms.

As it turned out, in the rioters' view most serious crime was committed by blacks who attained middle-class status and were living in mainly white areas. Blacks, forced out of their homes and apartments by their white neighbors, tried to escape in their cars, but were stopped at traffic signals, tollbooths, or even quickly erected roadblocks. Those halted—individuals, couples, whole families—were hauled out of their vehicles and beaten unmercifully. Most never recovered from the attacks, and many victims were unceremoniously killed on the spot. The number of casualties quickly mounted from the dozens to the hundreds, then—inexorably—toward the thousands.

Finally, running and pondering, I reached Central Park South. I continued north by way of some of the running paths I had come to know over the years. The park, usually well lighted, was now dark, most of its lights broken. I welcomed the cover of darkness, but not the pitfalls of branches, stones, and other obstacles I couldn't see. My goal now was not just to elude the rioters but to reach my apartment just above 100th Street. As I ran and dodged through the park, my building, where a good mixture of minority tenants and whites lived in harmony in an area that was now mainly black and Hispanic, seemed a haven.

Approaching my block, I could hear shouts on Central Park West. I climbed a hill onto a mass of boulders directly across the street from my home. A large group of rioters were just passing, heading south. Thank goodness, they weren't attacking my building. Then I saw why. On the outer door hung a big white sign, its large black letters all too familiar: **Nigger Free.**

When the rioters were out of sight, I climbed down from the rocks, crossed the street to my building, and banged on the door. The doorman was armed, as were the two security guards standing with him whom I had never seen before.

"Let me in!" I yelled through the glass. "You know me!"

Without opening the door, the doorman just shook his head.

"Don't give me that," I yelled, furious. "Where's my wife?"

The doorman searched through the message rack, then slid an envelope under the locked door. Glaring at him, I reached down for the letter. It was from my wife: "I'm O.K. Try to get to Convent Avenue near St. Nicholas. I think we will be safe there. Love, J."

I was both relieved and enraged. So much for expecting friendly whites to stand up for you in an emergency! I recrossed the street, reentered the park, and found a hidden place to rest before continuing my journey north through the park. If we survived, I could already hear my white neighbors explaining—and expecting us to understand—why, afraid that our continued presence in the building would bring destruction on everyone, they had complied with the mob's demands to put us out onto those ravenous streets. Oh, of course, they acted with the greatest reluctance, and only to save their families from the danger and almost certain death—to which they con-demned us, their neighbors, their friends.

Still angry, I pulled myself up, every bone aching, my clothes soaked with sweat. Convent Avenue was another forty or so blocks north, deep in West Harlem. The challenge at 110th Street, and again at 125th, was getting past the police who were massed there—to keep the rioters out of Harlem, they said, but their actions were clearly intended to keep the blacks in. I managed to slip by some unguarded barricades and talked my way past those at the more densely guarded 125th Street. Beyond that point, the streets were filled with residents and with blacks who had fled from other parts of the city. Like me, they had managed to reach Harlem safely, though their faces all reflected the ordeals they had survived. They were exhausted, their clothing torn, often bloody. War refugees in America, I thought. And we are all Americans.

I wanted to drop where I stood, but pushed on the last twenty blocks to the street my wife had mentioned. It's lined with lovely brownstones, where well-to-do blacks once lived, and some still do. It is also usually quiet, but tonight the street was crowded with people in various states of excitement, fury, distress, pain, and all of these combined. The area looked like a combination aid station and soup kitchen. As I started up the stairs of the address my wife had given me, I heard a most welcome voice calling me from the street. As I might have expected, she was in the midst of that crowd, helping those who were hurt, hungry, and simply exhausted. We embraced, cried a little; and after she made sure I was not hurt, despite my tattered condition, she led me up the stairs and into the house.

It was filled with exhausted people, all talking at once. Each person had a story equal to mine—or worse. Finally, our "war" stories trailed off, the voices stopped. We were all silent, overwhelmed with horrors witnessed and heard.

"We must never let this happen again," a man said with quiet determination.

Everyone nodded.

"We need to start plannin' and start doin'," a woman said, also quietly determined.

Again, a vigorous nodding of heads.

But, as I joined them, I wondered. How many black survivors of past racial riots—pogroms, really—have made similar commitments? Can their victims have been any less serious than any of the people around me that night? Or any more able to modify or abolish policies that underlie racial hostility that explodes this way?

Just then, a woman near me drew something from her bag.

"Look," she said, "at what I pulled off my building when they threw me out!" She held the sign high over her head. **Nigger Free.** The words were the same but were—in her hands, in that group of wounded, brave, resolute black people—no longer invidious.

"Isn't this," she asked, "more a symbol than a curse? The whites saw one meaning in them. We must see another! **Nigger Free** tells us we are niggers no more!"

Hearing her, recognizing that urge to elicit good from bad, I felt a quiet triumph. Before I could turn and share it with the others, the telephone rang. Nobody else seemed to hear it, so I reached out to answer. Picking up the receiver, I looked around and found myself back in my office. After all I'd been through that night, I knew who my caller must be.

"How goes everything?" Geneva asked.

9

∽

RACIAL ROYALTIES

Throw out the life line across the dark wave,
There is a brother whom someone should save;
Somebody's brother O who then will dare
To throw out the life line—his peril to share?
Someone who is drifting away.
Someone is sinking today.

—Edward S. Ufford

After Geneva's call that morning, the phone rang continually. I was gritty-eyed and felt bruised all over as though I had actually run that marathon the night before to escape a murderous mob in whatever past or future time Geneva had sent me. All the calls were from radio and TV programs wanting me to tell them how I felt about the proposed Freedom of Employment Act, about black people (including the secret group of blacks I belonged to), about being called a traitor to the race. Nobody wanted to hear any explanation of mine. Everyone wanted me to confess the error of my ways or to make an all-out attack on the blacks who were challenging my loyalty. I refused to bow to either demand. After what I'd been through, it all seemed unimportant, trivial even.

The telephone kept ringing. I ignored it. I turned on my

computer, typed out a general statement responding to the questions I'd been receiving, and E-mailed it to my secretary with instructions to use it to respond to any other media calls. All was suddenly clear. Civil rights advocates lurch from one crisis to the next, always reacting to the latest indignity, the newest threatening action. Frenetic response leaves no time for long-range planning or, more important, perceiving major dangers—like those I had witnessed last night—dangers that build slowly, quietly, and then explode without further warning.

Teaching offers me that gift of time for reflection if only I can avail myself of it. No time like the present, I thought. I filled my briefcase with my mail and left my office. Going out the front door, I wondered if my weary bones were up to the subway ride home. I was surprised to see Jesse Semple waiting at the gate.

"You picking up a client here?" I asked.

"You, Professor!" he said, opening the rear door. "Your dean called my service. I think he figured you might prefer to put up with me again than ride the subway."

"What are you talking about? What's wrong with the subway?" I asked, though longing for the comfort of his limousine.

"You'd have it pretty tough today, Professor, with your face all over the front pages of the *Post* and the *Daily News* as the black man who sold out his race. In what hole did they find those awful shots of you? It's like they give whatever picture they got the O. J. treatment—you know, make you look like mugger, thief, rapist all rolled into one neat, threatening package!"

"In other words, like a nigger."

"You got it! The tabloids don't want to confuse their readers with too many 'types' of blacks. Celebrities and criminals is the basic cut. The criminal types get the mugshot treatment."

I told Semple I was going home, and he headed west and north to the Hudson River. It was a nice day, he explained, and he thought my nerves could do with the calming of the river. The comfortable quiet of the big car did more than calm my nerves. I quickly dozed off. When I awakened we were passing Seventy-second Street.

"Oops! Sorry about that," I said. "It's been a busy few days—and night." I rubbed my still painful but evidently invisible bruises. "Since the dean is treating, why don't you take the Henry Hudson up to Riverdale and then we can circle back south to the 125th Street exit and head home from there?"

"How you doing with the media?" Semple asked after a bit.

"All they want is for me to confess that I created the Freedom of Employment statute for my own profit, or to attack my black colleagues who've challenged my loyalty—or both! Mostly, they just want me to be a contrite black man who has sold out my people."

"That's too good a story for those guys to give up without a struggle. Plus, white folks forever pressuring us blacks to act in ways that benefit them at our expense. Then when the shit you did for them comes out, they the first ones to point a finger and yell shame."

"You sure have the white folks down, Brother Semple, and," I added, "you do a pretty good job on us as well."

"I don't say nothin' you can't hear any day at a black barbershop." He looked back at me. "I suppose you don't go to one any more."

I shook my head, and explained that my wife's hairdresser, a Jamaican woman, cuts my hair about as well as has ever been done—though at twice what I used to pay. "But I do miss the barbershop conversations, the anecdotes—everything from politics, sports, women, and the lottery. When I was a boy, it was the numbers."

"Mostly the talk is lies," Semple said. "That's the problem with so many black men, specially young cats. They can't seem to be big and bad 'cept in the barbershop and the bedroom. We know what goes on in the barbershop is mostly bull, and the way these black women talk about us in the books they turn out by the dozen, we ain't all that much hell in the bed either. Though, makes me sick to hear these young studs boast 'bout they the father of three by three different girls. Like that's somethin' you want folks to know. It's hard for me to take."

"We *mustn't* take it, Brother Semple! The way things are today, most black men will be dead, in prison, or so hung up with anger as to be useless to everyone, including ourselves."

"Amen to that! 'Course I like what you say about this all-black group of professionals who meet in secret to plan racial strategy. Where the media see a dangerous conspiracy, I see a ray of hope. And it's good to know that some of you all doin' more than makin' money and livin' up to the bourgeois lifestyle."

"Well, at least one of the members is fearful I may interfere with his lifestyle—or so I judge by his leaking the story to the media."

"Who's that?"

"I promised I wouldn't reveal any of their names—including this man whom I'm afraid I provoked at the meeting. I'm sorry now, but I'm sure his leaking the information will come back to haunt him."

"You going into the retaliation business, Professor?"

"I sure am tempted sometimes, but I'll leave him to heaven."

"Humph! Heaven don't seem to be in the retaliation business, either—seein' as how the rich get richer, the poor get poorer, the good people die young, while the bastards live on year after year."

"Is that one of the old hymns you're quoting?"

"Yep, you caught me in a little plagiary."

He began to sing "Farther Along." I joined him in a rough harmony:

Tempted and tried we're oft made to wonder,
Why it should be thus all the day long,
While there are others living about us,
Never molested tho' in the wrong.
Farther along, we'll know all about it.
Farther along, we'll understand why.
Cheer up my brother. Live in the sunshine,
We'll understand it all by and by.

As we finished the chorus, Semple swung the car into a lookout along the drive. "I had another purpose in picking you up today," he said. Before I could protest, he waved a slim manuscript at me. He told me it was likely one of the manuscripts Geneva had left for him to give me on the trip we made several years ago. He found it later, then intended to get it back to me, but had forgotten it until the business about the secret black group came up.

"It's a story," he said, "about a secret black group who not only talks but acts on behalf of black people. Fact is, this 'Racial Royalties' story suits your situation now."

I hadn't an idea what Semple was talking about, but he wasn't a man to let me remain unenlightened for long. He proposed to read it aloud to me there and then.

"O.K.," I agreed. I welcomed the interlude and quickly relaxed in the sound of his voice and the beautiful view of the Hudson River and the George Washington Bridge.

∾

Initially the four long-time friends met to share their mutual misery. All were talented scientists and computer programmers. All had earned their reputations for skill and accomplishment. All, as well, were black and had found their progress blocked by glass ceilings while less impressive white co-workers were given promotions, higher pay, and recognition.

Kim Brown, a mathematician with special expertise in demographics, reminded the other three that their problems were small compared with those of blacks who merely contributed to the culture tortured cries of hate, despair, and self-destruction.

"True," Nat Benson, a computer programmer, replied, "but what do you expect, Kim, when no one will hire an ordinary black man but the local drug dealers? It's work that offers quick money, followed by arrest and prison if he's lucky—and death in the streets if he's not."

Kim shook her head. "But how can whites ignore the suffering and simply see gang colors, rap music, and the like as ghetto styles they can copy and bastardize into profit?"

"Exploitation's not limited to time or class," Nat said. "It happens in science, too, to us and others like us. And how much money or recognition did George Washington Carver receive for his agricultural genius, or Jan E. Matzelinger, who invented the shoe-lasting machine, or Granville T. Woods, who was responsible for the automatic air brake? Not much for any of them is the answer. I could continue all evening listing others like them."

Even so, it was white theft of black culture that most moved the group to anger and eventually to action. They had been meeting for some months. Given their commitment to science, they were using the meetings both to bemoan their state and to discuss their works-in-progress. While discussing race one night, Lela Blackstone, a physicist with expertise in anthropology, summarized a paper in which she identified and attempted to quantify the cultural expressions of blacks, Asians, Hispanics, and Native Americans to American culture. To conclude her impressive paper, she read Langston Hughes's poem in which he laments the theft of black culture.

You've taken my blues and gone—
You sing 'em on Broadway

And you sing 'em in Hollywood Bowl,
And you mixed 'em up with symphonies
And you fixed 'em
So they don't sound like me.
Yep, you done taken my blues and gone.
But someday somebody'll
Stand up and talk about me,
And write about me—
Black and beautiful—
And sing about me,
And put on plays about me!
I recken it'll be
Me,
myself!
Yes, it'll be me.

After the last "me," no one said anything for a moment.

Then Kim spoke. "Do you suppose any of those complacent black conservatives ever read Hughes's poem? Or any other black literature? Or witness our music or our dance? Or care about the hemorrhaging of our cultural talent without any acknowledgment or compensation? There ought to be a way to stop that!"

A lightning bolt struck them all at the same time: The Idea. Why not use the advanced technological knowledge they shared to devise a means of metering the greater society's use of cultural expressions of subordinated peoples of color? Through existing satellite technology they could develop sensitive electronic devices capable of monitoring "cultural accouterments." The focus would be on "cultural conveyers," companies that make recordings, publish books and magazines, design clothing, prepare foods, and in other ways profit from black culture.

The monitor would record how much a particular company

used African-American music, dance, dress and hairstyles, language, and so forth, and then charge it a royalty fee. These fees could be channeled into urban redevelopment projects that government now claimed were too expensive.

Whites would not pay the charges voluntarily, but the group's computer scientists felt certain that they could devise a means of tapping into the major data banks maintained by banks and credit card companies. The group pledged themselves to absolute secrecy about what they called their "CCC Project." And they kept their word. Until they placed it into operation, there was not even a rumor about it.

Between the inspiration and the final program lay months of hard work and more than a little sheer genius. For reasons that reflected their wry humor, they chose Labor Day to turn on the carefully constructed equipment. While all systems functioned, several days passed before corporations realized that anything was amiss. Then, as if on signal, there was a great hue and cry about computer theft. Large sums were missing, auditors reported, but could not discover where the money had gone. As the amounts grew, sometimes disappearing from computerized accounts before the very eyes of corporate officers, outrage turned to alarm.

At the same time, community groups working in ghettos and barrios and on Indian reservations began to receive grants from a hitherto unknown foundation. Recipients learned that they had to use the funds to advance the aims of programs that would provide real benefit to people whose aspirations and talents were ignored because of their color. Recipient organizations must file regular financial reports and not divulge the source of the funds. Most did so. Those who didn't found that the source of their new funds completely dried up. Many months passed before government agents connected the grants with the missing corporate funds. At that point, the original members of the CCC Project decided to go public.

With a public relations sense equal to their scientific skills, the group prepared a video report and delivered it simultaneously to major media outlets. This hourlong film began with Ossie Davis and Ruby Dee reading the Langston Hughes poem. Then with a series of MTV-style splices and montages, the film portrayed the often shameless plundering and commercialization of black music and culture and that of Native Americans, Hispanics, and Asians. In a brilliant segment, they made split-screen comparisons of the song, dance, fabric design or dress, or hairstyle as originated by blacks and other subordinated people of color with the rip-off versions that appealed to whites—simply because the performers or manufacturers were white.

Then the scene shifted to the CCC Project's secret headquarters, where members of the group, speaking in a conference room sufficiently dark to conceal their identities, explained that the formulas used in making various assessments were based on the royalty fees generally paid to writers, composers, and other artistic creators. They did not explain how they were able to continue removing those charges from corporation accounts despite the most elaborate efforts to protect them. Referring to these efforts, one of the group laughed softly and suggested that no one would succeed in halting their activities who did not truly understand jazz.

The final portion of the film was truly inspiring. It showed how the funds were being used to reconstitute lives and communities ruined by society's neglect and exploitation. As advocates had long urged to deaf ears, the answer to crime was not more police, more prisons, more repression. Rather, the need was for jobs at decent wages and the chance to develop skills to hold those jobs. The CCC funds had provided many of both, and the programs were expanding. The answer to the drug problem was not a war, but a declaration of peace. CCC funds made drugs available at no charge. One could obtain them openly on the street. With the market thus saturated, drug profits and the crimes motivated by them all but disappeared. At the same time, drug rehabilitation was easily available, with a thoroughly thought out support system.

"This nation has long urged people of color to lift themselves by their own bootstraps," one of the group reminded the audience. "Such admonitions were repeated even when the nation knew, or should have known, that the boots of many of those people were nailed to the floor by poverty, by lack of education, by racial hatred. We have simply done what the society urged, and we have done it on terms that, based on its history, the society should recognize—the involuntary taking of property. As victims of such takings throughout this country's history, we find it amusing that the nation now calls us thieves and condemns us."

At the film's conclusion, the group pledged that the assessments would end when people of color were valued equally and given the same life chances as other citizens. Any efforts to retaliate against the beneficiaries of the CCC assessments would automatically increase those assessments. And, the spokesperson added, the computers used to make the assessments were so programmed that if the group were not available to operate them, they would automatically send out a strain of viruses that would bring the nation's computer networks to a total halt. No one had to spell out how damaging that would be.

Finally, the group offered to halt the assessments if the federal government would enact legislation that would accomplish the goals of the assessment program through a program of royalties (they offered to show how this might be done). In addition, they wanted a commission established to study the history of racism in the United States, and make recommendations that would be enacted into law and enforced.

The group set no deadline for such action. Before the end of the telecast, phones were ringing in newsrooms, television studios, corporate headquarters, the offices of senators and representatives, and the White House. It was Orson Welles's "War of the Worlds" all over again—only real this time, and far more upsetting.

10

ɔ

WOMEN TO THE
RESCUE

Speak to my heart, Holy Spirit.
Give me the words that will bring new life.
Words on the wings of the morning,
The dark nights will fade away,
If you speak to my heart.

—New York Restoration Choir

"Brother Semple," I said, when he'd finished, "we need more dedicated black folks like those scientists in Geneva's story."

Semple nodded. "'Course," he said, "I'd settle to have someone like the woman who wrote the story." He cast a sly glance back at me, but I hadn't an idea what he was getting at, only that he was changing the subject.

"You know, Professor," he went on when I'd failed to rise to whatever bait he was casting me, "when Geneva Crenshaw dropped that bundle of stories off for you, I could see she was smart and sassy and one helluva good-looking woman. How long you two been goin' together?"

"Wait just a minute, Mr. Jesse B. Semple"—speaking as stiffly as I could—"I have been married most of the time I've known Geneva."

"So?"

I was shocked. "We are not going together, Mr. Semple, if you please! We have a close relationship, but it is not romantic, especially if you define romantic as including sex."

"Excuse me, sir!" Semple said with equal formality. "Guess I didn't know a man and a woman could have a relationship close as yours that was not romantic—and I do mean sex, and plenty of it!"

"Listen to me, Jesse!" I was really angry now. He had touched on a subject close to my heart for many reasons, and one I had thought deeply about. "How can black people ever rise above our subordinated state in this society if so many black men see our women, as you evidently do, as no more than sexual playthings? Black women may have good minds, great ability and talent, may even be good people, but none of that matters until you've gotten them into bed. And by giving sex priority over everything, you sow the seeds of alienation, not respect.

"It's like—like you're given a marvelous wood carving, and, instead of preserving and treasuring it, you see it only as good firewood."

"I see you feel kinda strong on the subject," Semple said quietly.

"I do, I admit it. It's not just Geneva, though you are far from the first man who has assumed our relationship is sexual simply because we are close. It is an assumption that shows you're likely missing out on some very fulfilling relationships with women."

"You're going to have to break that down for me, Professor."

"Listen, Jesse, it's not complicated. Because so many men equate women and sex, women have to always keep their antennae tuned to come-ons. When they realize you're really interested in them as human beings, you can develop friendships that are more valuable—and usually last longer—than those based on romance and sex."

Semple laughed softly. "I'm sorry, Professor, but I've been around the block a few times even if college wasn't on the route. You may not want to deal with it or—how do you college folks put it?—consummate it, but it sounds like a romantic relationship to me. And, excuse me, but seems I remember you were touchy during that trip up to Westchester when I told you a tall, black, and very handsome woman had left a large envelope for you."

"I don't remember being that way at all!" And I felt more than a little defensive as I spoke. "Geneva and I have known each other for probably thirty years, and worked together on cases in the Deep South during some scary times. Do I love her? Absolutely. I would do anything for that woman, and, she would, I think, for me. But we do not sleep together! Never have, and I doubt if we could be as close as we are if we were lovers in the way you mean. It certainly wouldn't work with me married to someone else." I glanced at Semple's blank face. "Am I getting through to you at all?"

"You want the truth? No! Professor, you are now way beyond both my schoolin' and my experience—and my self-control, if a woman like Geneva cared for me as much as she does for you."

"But, Jesse, that mind-set, especially since it's held by probably most of our men, could be the doom of our people in these perilous times."

Semple shook his head. "You tellin' me we black men got to give up our natures in order to save the race?"

"You have to give up the belief that the primary reason women are on this earth is to entice and satisfy what you call your 'nature.' Women are far more than sexual vessels. For a long time, I thought race and sex were separate agendas, but I have slowly come around to agreeing with my women students—white as well as black—who have been telling me for years that we blacks must deal with sexism and patriarchy in our communities before we can address effectively the continuing evils of racism. Indeed, black people must come to realize that our greatest strength—our survival hope, if you will—is black women."

Now Semple was shocked. "What are you sayin', Professor?"

"Somehow black men and women must see the essential need to accept and practice gender equality before we can fight effectively for racial equality. Failing to do so means we, we—" I struggled for an apt analogy. "It means we will keep on treating our women like so many whites treat us."

"That's strong, Professor, but I don't see the connection between racism and your sexism."

"Think about it, Jesse. Whites want blacks to stay 'in their place,' always subordinate, doing the dirty work, and not complaining and, whenever possible, making white folks feel good even if, in doing so, we feel bad. Many of our men want their women to perform in a similar fashion. It causes alienation and loss either way. Whites don't think they have to change. We can't afford not to!"

"Meaning?" Semple asked.

"Meaning, that the way it is now, black men and women are wasting much of their energies and strength—their human resources—in bitter enmity and recrimination. We have to stop it! We men must absolutely abstain from acting on the society's sexist and patriarchal assumptions and doing things that demean women. Those assumptions may seem natural, but they were imposed by the white culture. We don't need to swing all the way back to the matriarchal societies of our African ancestors, but we do need to find some middle way where we are equal partners with women.

"We black men must understand that black women are as likely as we are to understand what should be done and how best to do it in every aspect of our lives: business, educational, political, religious, economic, social, personal. Just as we acknowledge women's power to give life, we must come to recognize their power to sustain us in life, to play critical roles in planning and actions during the critical times to come. I really believe that!"

Semple sat quiet for some time. "You may be right," he said at last, "but I can tell you, you'd be laughed out of my barbershop if you came up there preachin' that women-should-be-in-charge stuff."

"Maybe that's a good reason for me to go."

"Maybe so, Professor, but listen. Could even the Good Lord Himself, at this late date, change the nature of human beings, and especially men's sense of what a man is?"

"It's not a question of nature, Jesse. It's one of mind, of will. I mean, my own sense of what a man is and what he should expect of women has evolved over time. What we need to do is open our eyes and consider what black women have done throughout our history. To what they are doing, or trying to do in our poorest communities. And, for the most part, they are carrying this burden alone. All too many black men are definable by their absence or their disruptive presence. Even men who are skilled or educated are often irresponsible when it comes to the commitments and sacrifices needed to sustain a strong family and a viable community.

"All true, Professor. But I hope you not forgettin' the many, many black men who are workin' their behinds off for their families and to do somethin' worthwhile in the world."

"Of course not. But it is also true that for a generation now, a host of writers—many of them black women—have been telling the world about the inadequacy of a great many black men. This often emotional testimony ranges from mournful frustration to flat-out rage. The revelations contain both deeply felt disappointment about what often is, as well as yearning hope about what might be. Again, while there are many, many black males who do not fit the woeful patterns, we know from statistics and personal experiences that the criticisms are far more valid than mythical."

"That's pretty cold," Semple responded. "Life for black men in this racist America is damn difficult. Sure, we mess up, but a lot of that messin' up's caused by the hostility we get every time we go out the door. I mean, listen," and he dove into his usual pile of books stacked on the floor beside him. "What makes this job worthwhile," he mumbled as he searched. "Lots of time to read while waiting for folks. Here it is!" He paged through a heavily underlined volume. "James Baldwin sure was tellin' the truth when he wrote that 'the action of the White Republic, in the lives of Black men, has been, and remains, emasculation.' And on the other side, I sure hope you haven't forgotten, not all black women are saints. Some of 'em are fools, connivers, self-seekers, and pardon the expression, pure-D bitches!"

"True enough. Men do not have a monopoly on acting foolish and being no-account—but, Jesse, don't you see, it's a vicious circle? Society beating on black men who, in turn, beat on black women who, in turn, vent their frustration and rage back on them—on the very people with whom they should be working, heart and soul, to break the destructive cycle.

"We exhaust ourselves with recrimination. This society has not much loved either black men or black women, and debate about whether society's hostility or black male rage directed back on itself has done the most harm doesn't move us closer to the relief we both need. And much of that relief must come through building strength within ourselves and our communities.

"Blaming all our failings on racism, Jesse, makes white folks the scapegoats they've made us all these years. The difference is they still have most of the power."

Semple nodded, but was far from ready to give up his

point. "Maybe we do blame too much of our failure on whites, Professor, but that's not changin' the fact that black men in America find it so tough to fulfill the basics of manliness: provide and protect family. This being the case, your urgin' that we black men simply give up our traditional role as provider and protector, or share it with black women, will be the unkindest cut of all in this society's devoted resolve to emasculate black men."

"Jesse, please! All I'm asking is for black men both to stop trying to emulate the white man's macho sexism and to work with women toward a more natural and healthy equality between the sexes, with each person doing what he or she can without regard to who earns what, who holds what degrees or none, and whose job or career is moving ahead faster."

"Seems to me," Semple said, "you describin' an ideal that very few white folks and no black folks likely to reach given what is given. Did you ever stop to consider, Professor, what you call 'macho sexism' may not be the invention of white men, but may come with the territory of being male?"

"And did you, Jesse, ever stop to consider that false images of malehood may explain why, out of frustration when we can't fulfill them, we fall back on the stereotype of black male as stud? Some black men, even in law school, boast about how many women they've taken to bed. And, while I am not out there, I don't need to be to know that many of the young brothers on the Avenue are boasting of how many girls they've made pregnant. I am sorry, but it's just awful!"

Semple exploded. "Man, I don't say what happens is right! I'm just sayin' you can't ignore the makeup of men, including their weakness for gettin' some you-know-what and for bluffin' and bullin' about it. Keeps their minds off all the ways they failin' to get themselves the money and power they need to make it in this racist country. Baldwin has somethin' to say about that, too"—and, again, he opened his book—"if I can find it.

"Baldwin writes about what he calls the 'universal mystery of men.' He says 'a man cannot bear very much humiliation; and he really cannot bear it, it obliterates him. All men know this about each other, which is one of the reasons that men can treat each other with such a vile, relentless, and endlessly inventive cruelty.'

"Now," Semple continued, "listen to him comparin' how women and men deal with humiliation. He writes that women 'survive and surmount being defined by others. They dismiss the definition, however dangerous or wounding it may be—or even, sometimes, find a way to utilize it'—"

"Precisely my point," I interjected.

"But men," Semple continued reading, "'are neither so supple nor so subtle. A man fights for his manhood: that's the bottom line. A man does not have, simply, the weapons of a woman. Mama must feed her children—that's another bottom line; and there is a level on which it can be said that she cannot afford to care how she does it.'"

Semple paused, then read slowly so I would not miss a word. "'But when a man cannot feed his women or his children, he finds it, literally, impossible to face them. The song says, Now, when a woman gets the blues, Lord / She hangs her head and cries / But when a man gets the blues, Lord / He grabs a train and rides.'"

"Baldwin makes your point, Jesse, and in his usual elegant style. And the truth is even we black men fortunate enough to provide for our families must defend against the myriad forms of emasculation the society has placed in our paths. Achieving success as this society measures it exacts a very real and often terrible price. The old folks talked about 'laughin' when it ain't funny and scratchin' when it don't itch.' None of us escapes the need—the absolute necessity—of doing the same thing in more subtle ways to keep white people from feeling threatened and acting on that fear. I mean, even those of us who feel we have established some limits to what we will put up with, spend far too much time criticizing those who, by our measures, have been too willing to comfort whites in order either to get ahead or—usually—to stay even.

"But I'm not talking about blame, Jesse. I'm talking about how we might have the best chance to survive our future dealings with white America. Your point is that men are protective about the male role as provider, as protector. But why can't they continue that role with women as equal partners, expecting them to provide and protect as well, rather than reducing them to subordinate roles where they waste valuable time and energy trying to get men both to do the right thing and to believe that right thing was a man's idea all along? All that's a charade, a male-female charade. More black men may come to gain a real respect for women as human beings and not always view them first (and sadly, for some of us, foremost) as potential sexual conquests.

"Viewing women as sexual objects isn't a failing of black men alone, God knows, but it's a deficiency in whatever man or community it occurs in—and a deficiency we black people can no longer afford. We must recognize in some of our women— many of them, really—the amazing combination of strengths that can transform our relationships and lead us, even in a permanently racist land, to more effective strategies for survival, even success. In academe, I think of women like Johnetta Cole, the first woman president of Spelman College, and Ruth Simmons, the first black president of Smith College. I think of all the black women college teachers and administrators who report their 'life ain't been no crystal stair' experiences in *Spirit, Space and Survival: African American Women in (White) Academe*. And this is only one of any number of areas where black women have shown us the potential if we men come to see what we have in our midst."

"Impressive, Professor, but I don't know. Those women students of yours might be wrong. Seems gettin' white folks to give up their racist ways may be a piece of cake compared to what you're taking on. Another thing, and don't get me wrong, but you talkin' out of your experience. You been happily married most of your life. Plus, you been fortunate enough to be able to work at good-paying, high-level jobs. You never been in the fix of not bein' able to provide for and protect your family. Not many black men can say that. So you should not be so self-righteous in tellin' black men not in your position how we should react when we can't put bread on the table or money in the bank. You don't know what you'd do if you were walkin' in our shoes. And you should go slow in preachin' what you don't have to practice."

I thought a bit, then acknowledged that he had a point. "I'll keep it in mind, Brother Semple. I'll keep it in mind. But I still say one can't define right by circumstances. Abuse is abuse. For a man to insist that a woman be his subordinate, no matter what, diminishes both woman and man. You are right, I have been very fortunate, but it is that good fortune that has allowed me to see a better way, and feel under an obligation to point out the potential to those less fortunate but no less needy.

"Also, as I've said, I'm concerned not just with equal rights but with racial survival in the most literal sense."

"You said that, but I still don't get the connection."

I reached for my briefcase. "For some time, I've been carrying around a clipping about an incident that impressed me with the character and courage women can display in a crisis. This particular crisis occurred during rioting in New Delhi, India, following the assassination in 1984 of Prime Minister Indira Gandhi by her Sikh bodyguards. Mobs retaliated by swarming into Sikh neighborhoods, burning their homes and stores, and capturing, beating, and often burning alive any Sikhs they found. The police, who usually in the past had acted quickly to quell such disturbances, were notable by their absence. Following a night of uncontrolled rampaging, a group of about 150 Indians, men and women, mainly of the professional classes, organized a protest against the violence. They decided to march into one of the ravaged neighborhoods and confront the rioters directly. Shouting familiar Gandhian exhortations for peace and brotherhood, they walked through areas strewn with the debris of carnage. They didn't turn away from thugs, but faced them down, engaging them directly in dialogues which often turned into extended shouting matches. Finally—and this, Semple, is what I want you to hear—the writer reported:

> Rounding a corner, we found ourselves facing a crowd that was larger and more determined-looking than any other crowds we had encountered . . . [T]his particular mob was intent on confrontation. As its members advanced on us, brandishing knives and steel rods, we stopped. Our voices grew louder as they came toward us; a kind of rapture descended on us, exhilaration in anticipation of a climax. We braced for the attack, leaning forward as though into a wind.
>
> And then something happened that I have never completely understood. Nothing was said; there was no signal, nor was there any break in the rhythm of our chanting. But suddenly all the women in our group—and the women made up more than half of the group's numbers— stepped out and surrounded the men; their saris and *kameezes* became a thin, fluttering barrier, a wall around us. They turned to face the approaching men, challenging them, daring them to attack.
>
> The thugs took a few more steps toward us and then faltered, confused. A moment later, they were gone.

"What those Indian women did, Jesse, exemplifies all I've been saying about black women: their capacity for simple courage, for mutual understanding, for the deepest rapport."

"Very impressive," Semple agreed. "You think our women'd do that for us?"

"They have been doing it for a long time. Is it asking too much for us to treat them as well as we ourselves, whom they're willing to save, want to be treated?"

"Not for me it ain't, Professor," he said, starting up the car, "but a whole lot of our young brothers need to hear what you sayin'. They also need to hear about those women in New Delhi."

We both took a last look at the Hudson River before heading down the 125th Street exit.

11

~

THE ELECTRIC SLIDE PROTEST

When I think about Jesus and what He's done for me,
When I think about Jesus and how He set me free,
I can dance dance dance dance dance dance dance all
*   night.*

—André Crouch

No one thought the Million Man March of 1995 would ever be surpassed. They were wrong. This, probably the most spectacular racial demonstration in the history of civil rights, captured unprecedented media attention. For a few days afterward, there was virtually no other news coverage. Even the generous time usually allowed sports and the weather was cut back to make room for eyewitness reports and in-depth analysis on the political, legal, moral, and social significance of this signal protest. But the best account of it is the one Jesse Semple gave his brother, who had been off on vacation in one of the few remaining places in the world that manage to get along without newspapers or television.

With the protest, my speaking engagements had doubled,

and I couldn't have met the demand without Semple to drive me from one to another. One day, in what was to be a longish interval between engagements, he asked if I'd mind if he phoned his brother, who had just returned, to tell him what he'd missed.

"Sure," I said, "and if you'll allow me to record your account, I think I will have something to share with others who, like your brother, missed this event." Semple agreed and placed the call. From my long acquaintance with his thinking, I had an idea that his report would be pithier than anything in a newsmagazine or on television. Also, it might provide some insight so far unavailable from any of the participants in the protest, who would say only that they were glad they had done it and would do it again whenever they "got the word."

∽

Man, it was something! I cannot believe you missed it—and, no way, no way in this world can I describe it to you. But, listen, because you are and have been my main man goin' all the way back, as well as my brother, I'm goin' to try to do the impossible. I'm goin' to paint a picture for you. What? Naw, man. You goin' to have to be patient. I can't give you no picky summary. You can get that on TV from the white folks, all watered down to comfort them and confuse us. This the real thing I'm tellin' you about. How those X-rated film ads put it? Unexpurgated.

O.K. O.K. It was a beautiful morning, late spring. In fact, it was the mornin' of the day when the Congress was all set to take a final vote on the Freedom of Employment Act. You know, the one to end affirmative action and, some people say, start black folks back on the road to slavery.

Well, early that mornin', black women of every description under heaven began gathering 'longside major thoroughfares and in front of government buildings. Women turned out early in at least twenty major cities across the country. Yeah. D.C., New York, Chicago, Miami, St. Louis, L.A. I can't name 'em all—and, if you let me finish, you'll see why namin' them ain't important.

Now get this. These women were young, old, and all manner of in-between. They were all the sizes, shapes, colors you can imagine—even if you let your imagination get carried away. Some of *them* were there, too. This wasn't no class thing. To tell you the truth, it wasn't a strictly black thing either. I saw some white women, Asian and Hispanic women. Learned later they were related to, married to, or going with black men. Mostly the women were black. Were lesbians allowed in? How the hell should I know? Women whose sexual choice is other women are still women, as you'd know if you stopped soakin' up all that Old Testament nonsense from those bullhorn preachers on Lenox Avenue.

But stop interruptin' with foolishness. What I want to say is, man, seein' all those women together gave the word *sisters* a whole different meanin'. It was somethin'. There were women who do day work, secretaries, factory workers, housewives, teachers, beauticians, businesswomen, doctors, lawyers. Yep, there were some street hustlers there and also some nuns in their habits. Some sheditty, society ladies and some who, if they didn't split verbs, couldn't use no verbs at all.

What they doin'? They were quiet and seemin'ly so spread out that nobody paid them no nevermind. If anyone noticed as more and more of 'em gathered, they didn't say nothin'. Police? Police didn't come until later and by then, nothin' they could do—'ceptin look foolish and act vicious, which of course some of them proceeded to do. But, I tell you, these black women were so natural, so drylongso lookin' that no one was upset or nervous, as often happens when they's more black folks some place than there is whites.

Those women near post offices formed orderly lines as though waitin' for the doors to open to buy stamps. Women gathered at bus stops look like they waitin' to go to work. Many of the sisters seemed to be walkin' toward markets, malls, or department stores with nothing more serious 'n shoppin' on their minds.

I mean, none of them seemed hassled or in a hurry. Their numbers, by this time, must have been in the hundreds of thousands—at the very least. They gossiped with one another, laughed, kidded, recognized each other and exchanged greetings across plazas, up on overpasses, down flights of steps. I mean—don't get me wrong—you could tell these were black women even if you was blind and could only hear 'em. No, man, not loud—just *black*.

What you say? Man, would you let me tell this story my way? Sure, I know these women probably facin' all kinds of financial trouble or man trouble or child trouble. Almost certainly, job trouble. But all that stuff seemed like out of sight, out of mind. These women did not seem to have a care in life, and their only desire seemed to be enjoyin' the good weather and one another. Bro, let me put it like this. Town criers, you know the jokers back in the olden days, the ones who carried a lantern walkin' through town yellin', "Ten o'clock and all is well"? Well, they gone now, but if on this one day they could return to their duties, they'd have scoped that scene and figured, "Ten o'clock in the A.M. Black folks is in their place—and all is well."

Now, in Washington, it was 10 A.M., the hour when Congress was scheduled to open its session. In Chicago, it was 9 A.M., 8 A.M. in Denver, and only 7 A.M. on the West Coast. No matter. Precisely on the hour, all of these black women across the country, and the black-connected ones I told you about, began—now get this!—hearin' in their heads a large band playing music for dancin'. And not just any dancin'. Every one of these women knew the music immediately. As one, they yelled in friendly recognition of the sounds they all knew and loved: "The Electric Slide!"

They screamed, cheered, and clapped their hands. Then, in one gigantic movement from coast to coast, they moved en masse into the center of the avenues, parkways, streets, plazas, entrances, and onto bridges, subway platforms, train stations, and airport passenger terminals. As they moved, they already doin' the Electric Slide, doin' it as only black women can.

What a sight! Man, what can I say? It was poetry in motion, but that's too trite. It was rhythmic readiness, but that's too suggestive. What you say? Oh, militant movement. Yep, maybe. That sounds better, but, man, there was a joy in the dancin', not part of anythin' militant. It was a soulful response to the music, all those women actin' together but also for their ownselves. In fact, what they were doing puts the word *movement* to shame.

Oh, come on! You know what I'm talkin' about. I mean if you've been to a black dinner dance or party where the people there are old enough to—well, old enough to know what's truly happenin'. The music can be live or records—makes no difference. At some point, the band or the disc jockey will play "The Electric Slide," and instantly, everyone—includin' those tired out from too much dancin', those who really don't want to dance, and, yes, sadly, even some who can't dance—everybody'll be on that floor. You hear me? *On the floor!*

Now, you know, this is no exclusionary thing. You don't need a partner to do the Electric Slide. Men and women, old and young, form lines, not formal, just what comes naturally. And, with no partner, you get in rhythm with the other people in your line. Or, if the spirit moves you, with the line in front or the one to the side—or, if the spirit really moves you, to whatever feels good.

Now, me myself, I confess I can't do the Electric Slide, hard as I've tried. My wife has tried to teach me, but I just can't get right either the moves or the rhythms. Yeah, it's a shame. And I only tell you this because you my brother. And also because, to tell the honest truth, I don't want to learn that dance.

I just want to watch it. When it comes on, I just slip over to the side of the dance floor, settle back, and enjoy myself. As you might guess, I do not watch the men, though some of them can go! But it's the women.

Don't get me wrong. This ain't no sexist or sex-motivated thing. I just love to watch our women move while they doin' the Electric Slide. Seeing them do that dance is like—well, it's like Liberation Time. Somehow, dancin' in those lines with everybody doing the basic steps, goin' backward and forward and turnin' at the same time—well, man, that gives 'em somethin' to work with. I mean, women especially like a routine, a structure if you will, somethin' solid as a base. Then, within that base, they sense a freedom to be free—to improvise like their bodies are musical instruments. And what I'm sayin', this is true of fly chicks from out on the Avenue and dignified judges, professional women, doctors, and legislators. They all get down, as we both know. Their expressions are too much. "Hey!" they're sayin' without utterin' a word. "Hey, World, this is me as I am right now! This is even me as I may never be again. This is about celebratin' me. Dig it? *Me!*"

O.K., so, you get the picture. Well, imagine that dance floor with the Electric Slide goin' by, spread out all over America on major avenues and intersections. As those women all began to move, traffic and everythin' else come to a stop. For a time, the white folks was mesmerized. Even most of them willin' to give us our due when it comes to dancin'. But then folks noticed that nothin' runnin', that everythin' backed up. And, you know it, white folks'd get upset if the Second Comin' kept them from gettin' to work to make that money. They'd grumble that the Lord should know better 'n to come back on a workday. And that, my man, is the Good Lord! All those black women, even with the white, Asian, and Latina women, didn't rate nowhere near the respect the Lord might get—that is, if He come back on the weekend.

The women don't seem to notice the growing commotion. The horns honkin', the shouts and curses. By now, they're into the Electric Slide as never before. And how does the gospel song go, "They ain't noways tired"? Well, the police wade into the groups and order them to disperse. The police get ignored, which no police like. Especially when the ignorin' is by black folk. Especially by black women. The police they gets mad and orders folks under arrest. But the women keeps on dancin'.

By this time, there's many more black women joinin' the dancers. Either they didn't get the word, which I hope was the case. Or, and this is what I would have to guess, they were just stone late. We're known to be late, especially our women when they goin' to somethin' other 'n work or church—as I do not have to tell you. Anyhow, late or not, the black women are fillin' all the public places both in the twenty cities where the thing started and now in hundreds of other places. And, as I say, they ain't even thinkin' about stoppin'. They just steady dancin' they behinds off.

Police reinforcements, including the riot squads, come out. First, they kinda taken aback. Then they start in yellin' threats over their bullhorns. Then, man, they wade in to clear the streets and intersections. The women get shoved this way and that, but they keep on dancin'. They don't even seem to see the police. So, if you can believe it—and I know you can—the police start using their billyclubs. Yeah, man! On the black women. But the women do not panic. They try to shield themselves by puttin' their arms up around their heads and dancin' in tight groups, but they keep dancin'.

By this time, as I've heard it told—not in the press, but by one sister who was there to another who was not—the music changed. As you know, the original Electric Slide recording had dance lyrics by Marcia Griffiths as well as plenty of melody and even more rhythm. Well, the rhythm slowed somewhat, and a really big gospel choir start singin': "I'm so glad, trouble don't last always." Sounded like the arrangement by Timothy Wright, the gospel singer. And the sisters start singin' along as they dancin'. Now, we can't hear the gospel choir, but the sisters is they own gospel choir—the movin', swayin' voices of thousands of women, mostly repeatin', "I'm so glad, trouble don't last always":

> He may not come when you want Him, but He's right on time.
> In times of trouble, he's a friend of mine.
> When the storm clouds rising, I know he'll be there,
> All your burdens, He will be there to share.

What? Yeah, man, I would say it, probably the biggest, baddest gospel choir in all of history! Something, man! Something!

Meanwhile, the police flailin' away, notwithstandin' all this gorgeous sound and in harmony which gives the women strength to face anythin'. When one of the sisters is hurt and falls, three or four other women stops and carries her over to the side, where black men and women, doctors and nurses, come out of nowhere and tend to the wounded. They carry out on stretchers those women needin' more medical treatment 'n they got on the scene.

The black men? Well, a lot of them, some caring for young children, are standing on the sidelines. And this is men from all walks of life—I mean *all* walks of life. Some got on fancy tailored suits and carryin' those attaché cases, others wore serving uniforms, others had lunch buckets, and a whole lot looked like they had no work at all. But they was there! They helps carry out the women who are hit, and they helps keep the children calm. But 'cept for a few brothers who lost it and had to be held back from wadin' in after the police, the men do not inter-fere with the women, even though some must be their sisters, wives, mothers, girlfriends.

It was powerful, man! Brings tears to my eyes just tellin' you about it. This protest was a black women's thing just like the Electric Slide's a black women's dance. The men knew it, respected it, supported it. But they didn't jump in, try to take over, or tell their women to leave. I've never seen nothin' like it.

Brother, give me just a minute here! I'm gettin' too choked up to talk. I ain't never in my life been so proud to be black. We ain't got much and gettin' less and less all the time. But we got heart, and we got soul. And both was out there and on dis-play on the streets and avenues of this damn country. Some-times I think we the only ones got it.

And what do we get? We get no r-e-s-p-e-c-t, as Aretha'd put it. They try to beat it out of us. And mostly they use the police to do it. The police? Where I was watchin', they gave up and stood by—in case the women should try to enter buildings and such, which they never did give any intention of doin'. The TV news reported that in other cities the police got carried away and fired tear gas into the dancers. Some women were overcome, but most just moved down the avenues, still dancin', until the police give up.

Yeah. Sad to say, there was some shootin'. Police now denyin' it was any of 'em did it. But even seeing the sisters fall did not stop the dancin'—though it did provoke some brothers to break ranks and go a little crazy. But even when there was a hullabaloo, the women did not even slow the tempo. They danced all that day and well into the evening. Men brought them sandwiches and drinks. And some of the older women would take breaks. But nobody left until it was over at 10 P.M. on the East Coast.

⁓

Meanwhile, back at the Congress, that mornin' they heard about the carryin'-on outdoors. Plus, all they could see out their windows was thousands of black women dancin' all 'round the Capitol building. What? Sure, they got nervous. Wouldn't you? They put off the vote. Claimed it was 'cause the dancin' kept a bunch of the congresspeople from getting to work. Savin' face is what they doin', if you ask me.

Bring the bill up for a vote tomorrow or next week? That's what they claimin'. Me, I don't believe it. White folks is stupid on race stuff, but they ain't crazy. They will think of other ways to harass us and keep us down. They already sayin' that protest is one thing, disruption another.

What? While clampin' down on the one, they'll sure as hell try to put a halt to the other—free speech or no.

What you say? Yep, black folks down there sure all fired up. Same here. Same everywhere, far as I can make out. TV not sayin' very much, but I have not seen so much plannin' and preparin' since the early 1960s. Men's groups say they want to do something just as big, and even the national civil rights groups claim they'll be leadin' protests and boycotts.

Yeah, it's easy to talk, hard to do. I think people serious this time. It's like back in 1961 when those four college students protesting segregation by sittin' in at that soda fountain in Greensboro, North Carolina, started somethin' that spread across the South, across the country. And they was only four, not four million. I think this Electric Slide Protest has started somethin', somethin' big.

What? No, Bro, I have not heard a word about the Freedom of Employment Act. In fact, I will bet you real money we do not hear of that bill again.

What? That much? You are on, man! I'll match my knowledge of white folks with yours any day of the week! Talk to you soon. And, brother, get your money ready.

12

~

EQUALITY'S CHILD

There is no pain Jesus can't feel,
No hurt He cannot heal,
All things work according to His perfect will.
No matter what you're going through,
Remember, God is using you,
The battle is not yours, it's the Lord's.

—Yolanda Adams

Cafe Beulah, the popular black restaurant in the Flatiron District of New York, was even more crowded than usual on Saturday night. As we savored the food—they call the cooking South Carolina low country—Jesse Semple was regaling us with his view of the Electric Slide Protest. My wife and I had invited him, Gwynn Gant and her partner, Meredith, and Geneva. I was surprised and touched at Geneva's willingness to engage in an ordinary evening with other people, though I am not sure whether she was pleased or annoyed that so many of Cafe Beulah's patrons recognized her and came over to thank her for her stories and ask for her autograph.

"See," I whispered to her, "I haven't, as you sometimes suggest, been taking credit for your stories." Geneva nodded. She was parrying our questions regarding the Electric Slide Protest.

She kept repeating that it was a great event for black women, and should be an inspiration, a classic example of a social gathering harmonized with political activism. She insisted that women's groups had done most of the organizing, that several women had suggested the song, and that her role was "purely one of coordination."

I realized that Geneva wanted this protest to be a black women's victory, not hers. I thought I saw another motivation in her refusal to take credit for what she had apparently done, one she likely would not reveal even to me—unless I pushed which, of course, I planned to do with a story of my own. As we dug into the impressive entrées, I let my mind wander. We had been very fortunate, I thought, counting our blessings, the many potential disasters that had turned themselves around.

Semple had won his bet. After the protest, a strong majority in Congress had ignored the demands that the country get tough on disruptive, but otherwise peaceful protesters—even if there were millions of them—and backed away from the Freedom of Employment Act, offering enough lame excuses to put that legislation on the permanently disabled list. Civil rights groups were declaring a victory, though none of their traditional approaches had had any effect whatsoever on that outcome. As for my status with the civil rights people, they had returned to their normal suspicion that I am not a team player and thus not to be trusted. I understand their reluctance to welcome me into their midst, but I am too old to change now and—alas!—so are they, or most of them.

In addition, the tabloids and TV newspeople have moved on to more juicy subjects—or, as likely, ran out of unflattering photographs. After following me around for a week, and checking my movements for God knows how long, they concluded— but certainly did not admit in print—that I was sleeping with only one woman, and I was married to her. Geneva, as I kept telling them, was my friend and colleague, and Gwynn was both a lesbian and a fine lawyer. It was, I kept repeating, quite possible to be both. Meredith seemed to be slowly adjusting to a life of being black by proxy and was entering wholeheartedly into this evening's festivity. All in all, the papers concluded that we were all too boring to live, much less be written about.

With the past taken care of, I turned my thoughts to the future. Black people are still threatened by the transformation of the American economy from one based on production to one based on the exchange of information and the use of high technology to replace workers. The steady erosion of the job market—as jobs simply disappear or don't pay a living wage or require special skills—can lead only to disaster: men and women and children hungry and without homes, angry and desperate; riots and other mayhem; horrendous black casualties. My mind returned to my fearful run through Central Park—and, on cue, my bruises began to ache.

"Professor Daydreamer, would you rejoin the party?" It was my wife reminding me that we were supposed to be celebrating. "And here you are looking like the world's coming to an end!"

When I explained what was on my mind, everyone groaned.

"I know you think I'm a wet blanket," I apologized, "but if some of my fears are realized, this wonderful restaurant won't be here ten years from now. If our friend the host is still around, he surely won't be owning it. And, of course, the only ones able to afford to eat here will be white, and the lucky ones at that. All of us blacks'll be gone."

"Gone where?" Meredith asked.

"In prison, in work camps, or dead!"

Semple turned to my wife. "Is he like that at home, too? Every place I take him, it's serious seminar time. Almost two weeks now, and we have not discussed one ball score, said anything about the weather, or otherwise talked nonsense. He does not even talk about the womens 'cept to lecture me about gender equality."

"I'm afraid so, Mr. Semple, though I don't like to admit it."

"Lighten up, Professor," Semple advised. "Life is short."

"Just what I tell him, Mr. Semple," my wife added.

I looked to Geneva for support. "Not from me," she said. "I agree with your wife, Semple, and everybody else who has to deal with you."

"And, of course, Madam Crenshaw," I chided, "you're a fine one to talk as you work full-time, crisscrossing the country coordinating a protest. A protest, I might add, that while exciting, could—like so many civil rights victories of the past—result in long-range harms that more than balance the short-run gains." I looked around the table at all those faces so dear to me. "In fact, folks, I wrote a story—yes, one on my own—about a person something like Geneva. Want to hear it?"

Everyone but Meredith looked faintly dismayed. "I didn't know you wrote stories, Professor," she said. "I thought you just took credit for Ms. Crenshaw's."

"Well," I said, "let's say she inspired 'Equality's Child.' I wrote it originally for a special public television series on the concept of equality, what it means to Americans, and later added another ending."

Geneva rolled her eyes toward the ceiling, then smiled sweetly and reminded us that Semple had asked her to preach the sermon at his church the next morning. "I need to leave early to prepare myself," she said. In my experience, Geneva was always prepared, so I ignored her objection and began to read.

∽

Large, diverse, freedom loving, the country was very rich, very powerful, very proud. Even so, massive disparities in income and wealth belied the commitment to freedom and justice contained in the country's basic legal documents. Minority racial groups were discriminated against by the majority, many of whom lived marginally because they lacked the privileges of the upper class. Women, too, suffered from a deeply embedded patriarchy. In truth, there was little tolerance for religious beliefs, cultural attributes, political philosophies, or anything that departed distinctly from what was deemed the "mainstream."

Perhaps because they appeared impervious to change, the citizens chose to ignore barriers of wealth, class, and gender. Rather, they adhered to the principle of equality while eschewing its practice. On the anniversary of the nation's birth, banners espousing equality were everywhere. Politicians openly proclaimed what was obviously not true: that in all the land there existed no barriers to advancement; that here all who would, could rise solely on merit. Few dissented from these equality proclamations, and those who did were scorned as unpatriotic cynics.

The nation's leaders loved to tell—and its people loved to hear—stories of individuals born into poverty who by dint of earnest endeavor became successful, famous, rich. When these Horatio Alger stories involved members of minority groups, they were taken as unanswerable proof that equality was a fact and that those who denied it were simply misguided malcontents.

But the slogans of equality could not alter the economic reality. The disparity between rich and poor grew and grew until the nation's peoples were divided between the few haves and the great multitude of havenots. There were those in the land who worked for social justice, but their well-intended efforts always met overwhelming resistance when they sought change that might alter the socioeconomic status quo.

Thus, no matter how ambitiously undertaken, poverty projects were able to deliver only food without nutrition, welfare without well-being, job training without employment opportunities, and legal services without justice. In fact, the minimum relief reformers were able to provide to the needy served mainly to curb their revolutionary impulses and thus ensured maximum stability for the already well-off.

Then the wondrous young woman appeared in the land. Somehow, and appropriately, her features reflected a most felicitous blending of all the country's peoples. Her long hair was the texture of silk, her complexion a luminous golden brown. She was about fifteen, tall, lithe, her piercing amber eyes seeming wise beyond her years. Her voice was like music, her laughter like swiftly running water in a mountain stream. She wore a roughly woven gown and thin leather sandals. She accepted food and shelter with those in whose midst she would suddenly appear. She claimed no family. When asked her name, she replied simply, "I am Equality's child."

She did not lie, for she had no family in the nuclear definition of that word, which was the only definition the people in this land tolerated. But Equality's child had a mother, and her mother was far from pleased that her daughter had, without permission, gone to this country and—as her mother feared— begun to use her special powers to interfere in the affairs of its people. She and her daughter were able to communicate across space, mind to mind, and thus she ordered her daughter to return. Her pleas went unanswered. The young girl viewed herself as on a mission of enlightenment. Her mother would be pleased when she saw all the good that her only daughter could do in this place.

Beyond the failure to obey her mother, the young girl was lovable and, at first, was loved. But that was before the strange incidents—tragedies, some called them—were traced to her. All too soon, the pattern became clear. The child would appear at the front door of an individual or a family who, captivated by her beauty and charm, invited her to visit. She would accept for a few days, never more than a week. After she left, her host or host family began to act in ways quite contrary to their normal behavior.

Those previously not known for charitable impulses began to give large sums to the poor, often to the embarrassment and chagrin of their friends and associates. Some who had abided, and even practiced, racial or gender discrimination became outspoken advocates of justice for all. A few examples will demonstrate these character changes.

There was the young accountant. Ambitious and able, he was known as Mr. Prudent because he weighed every action—indeed, his every step—to make the right impression, to avoid giving offense. But several days after a visit from Equality's child, it happened. The accountant's neighbor and longtime friend was regaling his country club's dinner party with a story about the various deceitful ploys he used to avoid selling his house to the highest bidder, a black family.

As the man wound up, Mr. Prudent stood up and, in front of everyone, denounced his neighbor's bigotry and those who were applauding his tricks. The next day, Mr. Prudent located the rejected black couple, persuaded them to file a discrimination complaint, and testified against his neighbor, who was held liable for substantial money damages. Within a month, the accountant had been hounded out of his exclusive neighborhood. His job, while not in jeopardy, was no longer a sure steppingstone to an executive position. Though he was an outcast in his community, the accountant was undismayed. "I was simply," he said, "carrying out the country's proclaimed principle of equality for all."

The personnel officer of a large law firm confronted management about sexual harassment. He pointed out that the firm's general statement espousing fair treatment for all was not preventing many subtle but offensive ways the men assaulted the women in the firm, and suggested a plan to cure the problem. But the managing partners rejected his plan because it would embarrass several lawyers and their clients. When the partners learned that the personnel officer had begun to implement the plan anyway, they summarily fired him. Using his knowledge of the firm's harassing tactics, he published an exposé which harmed both the firm's reputation and its business. Competing law firms that had permitted similar practices publicly condemned bias while privately scrutinizing their personnel for any disloyal tendencies.

A schoolteacher refused to automatically assign "troublesome" minority youth to a special education class. Instead, she organized the community to challenge the school's assignment policies. Denied promotion to a principal's position, she also faced disciplinary proceedings for insubordination.

A postal worker, dismayed at the number of homeless persons standing around the post office, determined to give them a portion of each of his paychecks in dollar bills. After the second such distribution, there were so many homeless persons around the building that officials ordered the postal worker to stop his charitable giving near his workplace. When he refused, he was suspended for insubordination.

Like the ostracized accountant, none of those who acted against bias and injustice, and then suffered for his deeds, was upset by the retaliatory actions taken against them. But the public in general was disturbed, a disturbance much aggravated by the revelation on a national television show that each of the individuals had been visited and embraced by Equality's child.

At first quietly and then under public pressure, law enforcement agencies launched a nationwide search for the child. She was, they said, "wanted for questioning." The search intensified when it was discovered that people embraced by the child became, as the media put it, "equality-active," able to pass on her passion for equality by embracing others. There were reports that she would sometimes appear in a household, or in an office, or at a school classroom—but now that she was known and her warm embrace feared, she was shunned. Her appearance caused panic and, in one public setting, a stampede in which several persons were injured.

Those embraced by the child, and many suspected of having been, were placed in quarantine at a remote, heavily guarded site. The action, supported by the courts, was deemed necessary to prevent the spread of the "equality affliction." Government lawyers defending the quarantine claimed that the "equality affliction" threatened to disrupt the public peace and stability.

The nation's highest court agreed. Its most liberal members joined in the opinion, observing sadly that a nation's most dangerous citizens are those who seek to implement rather than simply espouse the country's most cherished ideals. It was a deeply sobering statement, one largely acknowledged by a prolonged silence in the courtroom.

During that silence, the young girl appeared. She had eluded the most diligent efforts to find her. On sight, security guards rushed toward her. The court's chief justice stood, ordered the guards back to their places, and said to the girl, "You are welcome here, young lady. We are prepared to hear what you would tell us."

Thanking the chief justice, the girl approached the high bench and, in her clear, lilting voice, said, "Beyond its role as a conceptual ideal, equality serves two roles in the society. First, the elite can preach the wonders of equality to the poor, while knowing full well that class-based barriers will bar all but the most able and fortunate from advantages that the well-off take for granted. Second, most of those who suffer discrimination because of race, class, or gender bias—though knowing full well the cause of their oppression, but having no alternatives save violent revolt—continue to view equality as an ideal that they can use from time to time as a shield against the worse abuses.

face of society's demand for conformity. They are physically in prisons, yes, but their hearts are singing. Their souls are free. You must go and visit them, Mr. Chief Justice, you and all this court. You will find it an inspiration to see persons who are truly free. They know who they are and what they are doing."

"And you, young lady, who are you?" the chief justice asked.

"I am like those you have imprisoned. I will tell you what they will tell you. Each of us is Equality's child."

Then, feeling her task in the land was finished, having sown there the seeds of true equality and justice, the child closed her eyes and said the strange words that had enabled her to leave her mother's home and travel to this country she had so strongly felt needed her. But nothing happened. She repeated the words. Again, nothing.

She opened her eyes. She was still in the great courtroom, and now guards were rushing toward her. She looked up at the chief justice for help, but he sat immobile in his power. The guards seized her and took her to prison. She was told she would have to stand trial for her transgressions. In her cold isolation cell, she cried out for her mother to help her.

Faraway, her mother heard. By now her anger had turned to anguish. She knew what the girl would slowly come to realize. Her child was beyond her power to aid. She had committed the Great Transgression. Although those who dealt in the Far Away were empowered both to understand the foibles of his world and to seek to convey enlightenment, they were absolutely forbidden to make any direct attempt to alter the behavior of its citizens and, thus, their fates.

Equality's mother, knowing the penalty for the Great Transgression, immediately appealed to the Higher Ones for mercy for her daughter. The child, the mother pleaded, does not realize that, however positive and good her intentions, she has done great mischief to those she influenced. The Higher Ones

"True equality," she pronounced, looking aroun[d] those stern and righteous white justices, their blac[k] denoting their solemn power of life and death, "can n[e] realized in a nation whose peoples view wealth and st goals more important than justice and equality, and wh[e] laws are designed to protect vested wealth."

"Young lady," the chief justice interrupted, "if you [?] that, why do you influence men and women to risk the[m] for an ideal of justice you maintain can never be achieve[d]

"The impossible is merely another name for challeng[e] girl replied. "Those who commit themselves to real e[?] will find personal triumph even as they suffer public [?] Their risks, undertaken even in causes lost before th[e] launched, serve to reveal the hypocrisy of those who u[s] words of justice for selfish, self-serving ends."

"Your equality crusade engenders hatreds and confus[?] the land," another justice responded. "Those people you influenced are now in quarantine and will not be rel[?] unless intensive psychiatric treatment can cure them o affliction you have caused."

"That affliction, as you call it, was always with them, [?] was suppressed by a society they knew would censor its [?] tice. Now they are experiencing a satisfaction no therap[y] change. They realize as well, Mr. Justice, that the way to[?] true equality is never passive. Those committed to justic[e] others do not expect it for themselves. The safety you seek not be achieved by punishing long-suppressed yearning[s] equality."

"Your equality crusade is doomed to failure, you un[der] stand that," the chief justice warned.

"Do you, Mr. Chief Justice," she asked, "really believe those you hold in confinement have failed? Each of the[m] overcome deep fears and spoken out for equality in the [?]

were sympathetic, but reminded the mother that her daughter's wrongful exercise of power automatically canceled that power. There was nothing they could do.

Now, Equality's child's future lay with those in the land she had tried to reform. As with the case for reformers everywhere, that future would be dark rather than bright, filled with far more misery than joy. In her cell, Equality's child could hear, from across the Great Beyond, the sound of her mother weeping and calling her name.

∽

"Exactly, what we wanted to hear to cap a celebratory evening." Geneva gave me a knowing look as she spoke. "Is there a moral to your story with its far from happy ending?"

"Only that good intentions, even when endowed with otherworldly powers, do not guarantee good results and can bring about great harm."

Gwynn protested, "Surely, you don't mean that Equality's child should have paid attention to her mother and not taken the risks she did in an effort to make real the symbols of equality?"

"I've always supported reformist activity, Gwynn, but as I get older, I realize that the effort to give life to symbolic terms like *equality* and *justice* and *freedom* is not only difficult, which we expect, but may be a *mis*direction of our energies and hopes. None of them encompass the essence of human need. Rather, they are terms we try to equate with a good life, one without fear, threat, or domination. All too often, though, these symbols lack the potential for actually delivering our daily bread—meaning employment, shelter, education, health care, and real opportunity to develop talents into skills that will be duly recognized and rewarded."

"But, Professor," Gwynn replied, "aren't you always quoting Professor Patricia Williams, who views rights less as enforceable constitutional protections than as a pantheon of possibility? In that sense our belief in our rights gives them life and thus keeps alive our humanity whether or not those rights ever materialize."

"Professor Williams is describing what we do and the praiseworthiness of our efforts. She reminds us that our goal is not the achievement of rights—which may or may not happen—but the committed struggle, one we should seek to join. I am suggesting that even the advantages can come at too high a price unless we are careful to target our committed efforts at toppling the real barriers, not simply gaining the symbolic ones."

"It seems to me," Geneva said, "that Equality's child was trying to get the society to give more than lip service to the concept of equality. To that end, she accepted serious risks to use her presence and her ability to influence those with whom she spent a few days."

"Perhaps, Geneva, but her approach failed to win the populace over to practicing their equality precepts."

"I thought you understood, friend, that the road of disciples and prophets is always hard."

My wife intervened at that point, reminding us that Geneva wanted time to prepare her sermon. We said good-bye to Gwynn and Meredith, who hailed a taxi to Brooklyn. Semple drove the rest of us uptown.

In the car, Geneva said that she wanted to speak to us all in confidence. "While," she said, "I do not accept the moral of the Professor's 'Equality's child' story, I am finding the road of activism itself quite difficult. The Electric Slide Protest was my first effort to move beyond stories and actually influence events." Ignoring my muttered, "I thought so," Geneva explained that her goal was to show black communities how to move *away* from sexist and patriarchal notions and actions and *toward* gender equality.

"And," she continued, "considering how resistant both men and women are to changing traditional sex roles, how little they attend to the lessons of my stories, I've decided to intervene again. Such activism is, as I suspect the Professor knows, absolutely forbidden to my Curia Sisters and myself."

She sighed, and in that sigh I sensed the awesomeness of some risk beyond imagining.

"The fact is," she went on resolutely, "that after this second effort, I may have to leave for a long time—perhaps forever."

"What have you done, Geneva?" I asked, truly alarmed.

"The only thing I can say now is that it may alter access to sex for many black people."

"Damn!" my wife said.

Geneva patted my wife on the hand. "That pretty well sums it up," she said.

We rode the rest of the way home in silence. As my wife and I got out of the car, we invited Geneva and Semple to come up for a last brandy.

"No," said Geneva, "I want to be on my way. Mr. Semple knows where to drop me off. I will see you both at church tomorrow."

Just before Semple pulled away, Geneva called my wife back to the car and whispered something in her ear.

"Want to know what she told me?" Janet asked as we went up in the elevator. I nodded. "She said, 'Take good care of him. He's trying to be a good person, but his efforts make him vulnerable. He needs a lot of help.'"

"And do you agree?"

"Of course. That's why I married you."

13

⌒

THE ENTITLEMENT

There are some things I may not know,
There are some places I can't go,
But I am sure of this one thing
That God is real.

—Kenneth Morris

If happiness can be equated with acquisitions, Donnell B. Dancer was a very happy man. He—as he often boasted—had it all. Luxury apartment, fine car, fancy clothes galore, a bank account replenished as often as it was emptied, and a seemingly endless procession of the most stunning women all these advantages inevitably attract. Donnell—everyone called him "Donny B. D."—referred to these women, though not in their presence, as "showpieces."

As important as money and what money can buy in late-twentieth-century America, Donny also craved celebrity. After years as a so-so show business performer, he had that as well. Donny was the good-looking, jive-talking host of the syndicated television talk show, "Let It All Hang Out," which was a hit from its first week. Five afternoons a week, the show featured interviews with a steady stream of people, mostly black, talking about their sex lives. The plan was simple: to give his audience of middle-class housewives and college students, and people hanging out in cafés and bars, every imaginable verification of all the myths about black sexuality—and then some. This was not a new idea. Several of the network talk shows had similar themes. Donny B. D. did them one better by ensuring that all his guests were either blacks talking about one or another aspect of sex or interracial couples—always a turn-on for his viewers—doing the same.

After little more than a year, he was right up there in the ratings with Geraldo, Jenny Jones, Richard Bey, Ricki Lake, Sally Jessy Raphael, and Montel Williams. Fact is, Donny considered himself better than his competitors, who sometimes presented guests who talked about something other than sex. That's why he was really pissed when that black sister Jill Nelson published an article on talk radio in the *Nation* and didn't even mention his name. Hell, his guests were dealing with all the stuff she described in her article: "mate swapping, men who beat women, fat women who are porno stars, the superiority in size of black men's penises, transvestites, men who don't support their children, ... people who love to have unprotected sex, ... white women who love black men, strippers, black women who love white men."

He had meant to write and complain, but he was too busy. Plus, he was getting plenty of print from real magazines like *People* and *Jet*. Mention in those mags helped the ratings. Plus, it attracted more of the kind of guests whose stories boosted the ratings even more. Donny B. D. laughed to himself remembering the two white girls who actually got into a fistfight on camera over which of their black boyfriends was the best lover. Actually, they were yelling, but didn't exchange blows until he brought out the boyfriend of one of them, and that boyfriend turned out to be—much to everyone's shock except his own— the man both women were boasting about. Funny, the two women went at one another, not the man. The audience ate it up.

Donny's show featured young black studs bragging about the number of "bitches"—usually teen-age girls—who had had their babies. Or, young mothers who claimed that nobody cared about them, including the children's fathers, and that having babies would give some meaning to their lives. Or, people who talked about the nitty-gritty details of every imaginable love triangle, even a quadrangle or two. Or, women who explained that they had given up jobs as secretaries and beauticians because they could make more money selling their sex. The show was as hot as the FCC would allow, and probably a lot more, particularly when Donny's male guests bragged about beating up and otherwise abusing women who still came crawling back for more of their "once in a lifetime" loving.

Donny expected the show to go on forever, or at least long enough to challenge Donahue and Oprah. That's why he was so damn mad the Monday he arrived early at his office all set to prepare for that afternoon's show, and in comes this raggedy-ass messenger with a letter from the station manager. Two sentences to tell Donny that the show has been canceled "effective immediately."

"He can't do that, can he?" Donny was screaming over the phone. His agent, upset himself, was trying to calm Donny down.

"I am afraid he can, Donny. It's in the contract. Plus, Donny, what else could they do? None of your guests have shown up for two weeks, and your ratings have dropped through the basement."

"So what! It's just a little slow, man! I can keep things going with jive talk till the guests start comin' back. We need to pay them more. Gettin' a chance to tell all their private business on TV don't hold the appeal it once did. But if the network talk shows can pay big bucks, so can we if that damn station would get up off some of that money my show's been pullin' in."

Donny's agent was quiet. There was no reasoning with his client just now. The show's producers had been offering double the usual rates for appearances. There were no takers. The agent understood that all the other talk shows were having the same problem—at least, with their black guests. "I'll see what I can do, Donny. Call you back."

"Wait! Wait!" Donny shouted. "Don't hang up." The receiver clicked. "Damn him! He'll pay for that."

He slumped down in his ultradeluxe office chair and sighed audibly. His irritation had not affected his mind. He might yell, but he had not gotten where he was by being a screaming maniac. He knew as well as the agent and the station manager that something was amiss. This black sex thing was a winner. White people, going all the way back, had transferred all their most base feelings onto blacks. Out of whites' demand for dominance came all of these sexual fantasies about the blacks they dominated. And, as the ultimate mark of their oppression, many blacks accepted this racist view of their personhood as basically a matter of sexual prowess. Exclusion from many of the job and career opportunities that help define who one is, contributed to the willingness of some blacks to live out the society's sexual stereotypes.

Donny knew all of this, simply by growing up in a Detroit ghetto. He didn't pass judgment on it, he simply wanted to get rich from it. His father had taught him that. "A smart man doesn't just enjoy sex, he exploits it." Now, all of a sudden it seemed to be ending, at least for black people and those whites married to or otherwise having sex with them. Donny shook his head. It made no sense. But, just maybe, the thing he had been experiencing for a week or so, was happening to others—scaring them as much as it had him. And, if it was, he could sure as hell understand why they didn't want to talk about it. He certainly didn't. It was too damn upsetting, to say nothing of embarrassing.

Donny's intercom interrupted his thinking. "Mr. Dancer, it's the reporter from *Essence* magazine here to interview you. Her name is Curia, and you promised her a half hour. Shall I show her in?"

Donny hesitated. Ordinarily, he would have welcomed a story in *Essence*. With its holier-than-thou editorial policy, the magazine had been critical of shows like his. Now, he thought, what the hell? "Show her in." *The way things are going, I may not be able to even buy publicity.*

Ms. Curia—G. C. Curia, she said her name as she extended her hand—was the kind of black woman Donny recognized instantly and just as instantly dismissed as "too serious." Smartly dressed in a conservative navy-blue suit, briefcase in hand, the tall, dark-brown-skinned young woman with her large horn-rimmed glasses looked to be a graduate, three or four years before, from an Ivy League college determined to make it in journalism and then write the novel that would put her name on the literary map.

"Thank you for seeing me, Mr. Dancer. Is this an O.K. time to talk? I just learned about your show's being canceled."

"And *Essence* sent you here to rub it in?"

"Not at all," she said, somewhat coldly. "I asked for this interview two weeks ago. But," she paused, "there may well be a connection between your show's cancellation and the S.E.T."

"The S.E. what?"

"We at the magazine working on the story have dubbed it 'S.E.T.' for Sexual Entitlement Therapy."

"So what the hell is it? And what does it have to do with my show?"

"That's what a team of reporters from *Essence, Ebony,* and *Emerge* are trying to find out. So far we know that couples began experiencing the S.E.T. several days after the Electric Slide Protest. At first, people didn't talk about it, but finally some confided in close friends, on the condition of the strictest confidence. Then shocking reports began to leak out. When black women are approached for sex by husbands, boyfriends, girlfriends, or even casual pickups, many—but not all—are prevented from carrying out their desires. The same is true when wives, unmarried women, or gay men initiate the lovemaking. The fact that one partner is not black does not prevent the S.E.T. from striking in otherwise appropriate situations."

Donny noticed the matter-of-fact manner in which Curia spoke about this S.E.T. business. He was impressed. She was professional and articulate. "What else have you learned?" he asked.

"Well, it has proven a real stopper in abusive sexual relationships. And, as far as we know, most prostitutes and participants of both sexes in 'porno' films have been unable to practice their profession. Virtually all unmarried teenagers are barred from having sex by the S.E.T., as are those who are H.I.V. positive, unless they or their partner is practicing safe sex. And, let me see, S.E.T. seems to have halted all rapes and coerced sex in which a black person was either the aggressor or the victim. Incest has become impossible. S.E.T. even seems to interfere with prison rape, though unfortunately not with the many other physical abuses that occur behind prison walls.

"There are other unexpected and, for the most part, unhappy aspects to the S.E.T. For example, gay and lesbian couples who had maintained that their sexual relationships were no more unnatural than those of heterosexual couples, gained a proof of their argument that many would have just as soon done without. In fact, until it became known that S.E.T. could affect all forms of lovemaking, homosexuals feared that a society notoriously hostile to them had come up with some new and particularly vicious technological means of 'gay and lesbian bashing.'"

Donny was listening intently. "Your magazine must love this thing, whatever it is. Why haven't the white media gotten a hold of it? Sounds like it would be the story of the year."

"Not many whites have been affected, and, Mr. Dancer, as something of an expert in this area, your guests are the black or interracial couples who would likely be having the S.E.T. experience. We thought you might have heard about it from them. We haven't gotten much data on its incidence because most people don't want to talk. Understandably, don't you think? Inadequacy in any area of life is tough to accept, even hard just to acknowledge. And, for reasons easier to comprehend than describe, the failure or inability to have sex translates all too quickly into feelings of inadequacy—regardless of the real cause."

"You're talking like some college textbook, hon—I mean Ms. Curia. It's not true. My program was a hit because black people were more than willing to come on and put all their most intimate business dead in the street. Now, to turn down a few minutes on the tube plus a free trip here from wherever, something must be scarin' the livin' shit—excuse my French— out of these folks. So, what have you heard?"

"I have our latest findings in my notes." G. C. Curia opened her briefcase, ruffled through a thick pile of papers, pulled out one, and read: "Couples contemplating consensual sex who are struck by the S.E.T. have basically similar experiences. They disrobe or otherwise prepare for lovemaking. Then, just as they are 'getting it on,' as some told us who may be more versed in the act than in its articulation—"

Donny laughed, then excused himself. "A good line. I'll have to remember it. Please continue."

Curia barely smiled at the interruption. "At the crucial point all their movements toward one another meet not the softness of a human body but the flinty surface of an invisible shield that has somehow slipped between them. No matter what they do or say—even scream—the shield is unyielding. And as they struggle, each partner—no longer a couple—hears, from nobody knows where, a gospel choir singing softly and a cappella. The melody is clear and hauntingly beautiful, but the lyrics are muffled. The baffled men and women can make out only these words of admonishment: 'You got to earn the Entitlement.' "

Donny, a veritable master of cool, almost lost it. He coughed to cover his discomfort. "I guess that's enough to scare a helluva lot of folks into takin' vows of chastity."

"That's not in our reports, but we estimate the S.E.T. has frustrated a lot of passionate people in bedrooms, hotels and motels, on living room sofas, in the backseats of cars, even on rooftops and in cellars, alleys, and hallways. Initial embarrassment is all too often followed by accusation. Accusation by anger. Anger leads to hateful words. But for the invisible shield, the anger—many women tell us—would be followed by blows. Efforts to break through the shield set off a sort of electric shock that both stings and chills any remaining sensuality. Some people try to defeat this invisible barrier by running around it, climbing over it, or crawling under it. We gather they look pretty funny, particularly given their various states of dishabille, but soon learn that a willingness to look foolish does not enable them to reach their partners to either hit them or go back to lovemaking."

"Hey, some of those couples would have made dynamite guests on my show! But is this S.E.T. thing happening to all black folks?"

"Yes and no, Mr. Dancer. It appears that all black couples hear the music, but many couples—evidently those in healthy, nonabusive relationships—experience no barriers. The gospel music serves as a pleasant background, even an enhancement of their sexual activity. These reports add to the frustration of those visited by S.E.T., interrupting what many deem the most important part of their relationships—yes, even their lives. When they learn that other couples—most of them married or in long-term relationships—are continuing to make love without the difficulties they are having, they really get upset."

"I assume," Donny asked, "that this S.E.T. thing hits even those who fall in love at first sight?"

"Not necessarily. Our reports show that sex, even on a first date, is still possible where the lovemaking is mutually agreed to and not marked by either dominance or manipulation."

"I bet I know what the S.E.T. victims do when they learn that some people are exempt. They start blaming their partners. Right?"

"Unhappily, your guess is correct. Once they understand S.E.T. is not universal, many men—yes, and some women—conclude that the fault lies with their partners. The solution? Here, as has so often been the case for reasons hardly the equal to this one, individuals constrained by the S.E.T. decide that the solution—"

"I know. Find a new sex partner. And it doesn't work, does it?"

"Not even for those who already had another sex partner—or partners. In this instance, having a spare or 'something on the side' almost never results in anything but more of the frustration they had already experienced with their primary sex mates. Setting out to make new conquests does not seem to work either. The investment in time, money, and effort leads only to sensual frustration rather than sexual success—a matter of no little discontent for those who considered themselves master practitioners in the art of seduction."

Donny was, by this point, looking uncool and uncomfortable. His tie was undone, and he was perspiring heavily. "Well,

Ms. Curia," he said, struggling to regain his composure, "now I know what happened to my guests, my audiences, my ratings, and my show."

"Since your program was all about sex, Mr. Dancer, I am surprised you have not known what was happening. We at the magazine are hoping you can add something to our data base."

"Well, I still find it hard to believe, except that since it's only happening to black people, the white folks must be behind it. They've done us a lot of dirt, but this is the absolutely worse—"

"We don't think S.E.T. is some kind of racist prank, Mr. Dancer. On the contrary, it seems to be some strange, even supernatural phenomenon intended to help black people get themselves together."

Donny shook his head. "Damn, sister! You sure are working for the right magazine. You sound just like one of *Essence*'s In the Spirit editorials."

"Maybe so, but just listen to this and tell me what you think. What our reporters are finding—admittedly only after a great deal of detective work—is that couples whose sex lives are interrupted by the S.E.T. are in relationships that involve serious physical and emotional abuse, adultery, bigamy, gross mistreatment, or exploitation. Couples where the men have deemed themselves 'in charge,' and thus entitled to dominance on all matters, are usually affected, as are women who feel that marriage or sex entitles them to being taken care of without any corresponding reaching out on their part.

"On the other hand, the sex lives of couples whose relation-ships are grounded in both shared feelings of respect and an equality of rights and privileges are not affected adversely. Small failings do not subject these relationships to S.E.T. inter-ruption. Compromise of differences seems to strengthen these couples whose relationships involve true give-and-take, not demand and submission."

"So, what's the bottom line, Sister Curia? Blacks can't have sex until they get sainthood?"

"Not quite, Mr. Dancer. But the reporters working on this thing find, that as a result of S.E.T., sex for black people is no longer a right, as many men believed. Nor is it an obligation, as many women had concluded. Blaming racism does no good—though racism has undoubtedly contributed to stresses that lead to negative behavior. There is no relief in civil rights law for those afflicted. And, as many are learning the hard way after the expenditure of more money than the *Ebony, Emerge,* and *Essence* editors are able to ascertain, no help is available in either medical science or in the old or new rostrums that are quickly flooding the marketplace."

"Right, right! I know damn well what won't work. Tell me what will?"

"Like it or not, Mr. Dancer, lovemaking for black people is no longer a matter of ability and appeal. It is an earned privilege, or what the staff is calling 'the Entitlement.' Sexual fulfillment has to be deserved, and is the result of loving treatment flowing in both directions between two people who honestly love and respect one another. The Entitlement can, we are finding, be lost by outrageous behavior and regained by a return to the fundamentals of gender equality—though the recapture is far more difficult than the loss."

"Sounds very boring!"

"Maybe to you, Mr. Dancer, but a great many women—and some men—see it as a godsend. And not all the reaction to the S.E.T. has been negative or destructive. If this thing continues, several black civic and church organizations are planning to lobby to amend existing social welfare laws. They predict, for example, that there will be a precipitate drop in teenage pregnancies, and want to redirect the resulting savings from the Aid for Families with Dependent Children fund to enhance aid for teenage mothers, including child care and educational assistance. Educators in public schools and after-school programs are considering courses intended to provide prepubescent young people with the principles of gender equality and really prepare them for the demands, as well as the rewards, of marriage. Existing black men's groups and new ones springing up are sharing their experiences, listening to family experts, and edging their way toward new understandings of their roles as men at home, on the job, and in the community. Black women's groups are providing a similar function. There is some discussion of 'outreach' sessions that will bring men and women together to explore and test the new relationships.

"So, Mr. Dancer," G. C. Curia wound up, "what do you think?"

Donny, his head cupped in one hand, was deep in thought. "Seems that somebody or something has decided to exploit sex for what they or it think is a good purpose, instead of personal profit. There may be an idea in there for a new show, but if you want my views for your survey, I'll be glad to give them."

The reporter got out her pen, pad, and micro tape recorder. "All set, Mr. Dancer."

"All this S.E.T. stuff must sound good to you, Sister Curia, and I'm not denying a lot of bad shit goes down around sex, but I don't think anybody should mess with Mother Nature. I mean, you just can't go around depriving individuals of their God-given sexuality. It's as much the right of a person as breathing and eating. Sure, you women bitch about sexism and—what do you call it?—patriarchy. O.K., O.K! But it's not right to do this just in the hope—in the hope, mind you—that black men and black women will get along better. The price is too high.

"This is the U.S. of A., sister. White folks been castrating black men, physically and mentally, since the beginning of this damn country. It ain't accidental that so many lynch mobs cut off or mutilated their black victims' sexual organs. Today the white folks do the same thing economically by cutting us out of jobs we need to support families and keep some bit of dignity. Now some supernatural force trying to be helpful has up and done the white folks' work for them.

"This S.E.T. thing is wrong, and it is wrong-headed. It sounds even-handed, but it operates on the basic assumption that men are sexual predators, and women compliant and submissive. I mean, sister, men ain't all that bad, and women ain't all that good! And sexual shit is far more complicated than that gospel group singing about you got to earn the Entitlement. You understand what I'm saying?"

"It is complicated," Curia acknowledged, "but it is too often abusive and exploitative as well."

"Well, even if this S.E.T. brings about an end to all sexual abuse among black people, that wouldn't end or even reduce the racist crap black people have to live with every blessed day of their lives. Given all the stuff the conservatives are layin' on us, it makes no sense to mess with our sexuality. Plus, we black men did not invent sexism and patriarchy, so if these things are so bad, how come blacks getting punished for copying the white originators, who are going scot-free?"

"Perhaps it's because, as you admit, blacks use sex to compensate for their lack of money and power. So the problem in the black community may be more serious."

Donny shook his head. "Now, sister, I can see you don't agree with me. That's O.K., too. Hell, I don't claim to be a prophet. I can be wrong, too. But this is supposed to be a free country, where laws are made by the people we elect. I do not recall any candidate promising to put this S.E.T. into effect, if elected. And, sure as hell, nobody asked me or, I gather, anybody else whether this was a good idea. We black folks have to fight capitalism by day and the dictatorship of some unknown hand at night.

"That's pure-D wrong, Sister Curia. And, I will continue to

believe that even if it means I never sleep with another woman in life—which, given my personal experience in the last week or so, may well be the case."

At his aggrieved admission, Curia looked up from her notes. "Yeah, it's true! I didn't know what was happening, and like everybody else, I thought it was only me. But it's not right, and I'm going to fight it any way I can! That's all I got to say."

"You have been around for a long time, Mr. Dancer. I respect your position, but—well, can I have a few more minutes to respond?"

"Sister, I've a lot more time than when I set this interview. Speak your mind."

Curia put away her tape recorder and notepad. "Mr. Dancer, even as a fairly sheltered co-ed, I found myself in situations that would—were I willing to make them public—earn me a guest spot on your show. And these were not just ghetto studs, but middle- and upper-class college men and women, white and black, who see sex as a power thing, a get-over thing, a prelude to domination, a means of proving manhood, womanhood.

"I believe the S.E.T. you and so many black people have experienced is less about sex than it is about our survival as a people. This most drastic treatment was intended to get us to see the need to restructure our spiritual selves, to rethink what life is all about, and to bring into harmony all the forces of our being, forces that bespeak our basic humanity and the miracle of our lives.

"Human sexuality, viewed as a God-given right—as you put it, Mr. Dancer—leads to all manner of abuse, a lot of which you had on display on your program. As a young black woman, I found it disgusting. Sex should be the reward for achieving full personhood, instead of a substitute for it. Engaging in sex without honestly caring about one's partner leads eventually, if not sooner, to despair, not bliss. It leads to exhaustion, not exaltation; to heartache, not happiness; to disappointment, not deeper affection—"

"Watch out, Jesse Jackson!" interrupted Donny. "This woman's stealing your thunder!"

Ignoring him, Curia went on. "And there's a political component at work here. Our reporters found that those penalized by S.E.T. tend to be politically apathetic and socially uncaring. Evidently, only when our hearts are in play can our minds fully open to the needs of those around us and to the dangers that threaten. Your program provided a daily parade of people who are being torn apart by behavior that is misogynistic and otherwise destructive of self and of those they abuse.

"The S.E.T. is, as you say, strong medicine, but it provides a unique motivation for reviewing and reforming attitudes toward one another.

"Mr. Dancer, rather than continuing to exploit the myth of black super sexuality, why not put on a program devoted to the Sexual Entitlement Therapy phenomenon? You might well find even more listeners willing to undo the myths that have robbed them of their humanity as well as their entitlement to sexual fulfillment. Think about it!"

For once, Donny did not even try for a sassy response. "Well said, sister," he said quietly. "Well said! You just might have an idea there!"

Curia picked up her bag and held out her hand. "Thanks for the interview, Mr. Dancer. And thanks for listening." But she didn't head for the door. She gave Donny a sly smile and then slowly dissolved into nothingness right in front of his widening eyes.

14

∽

THE GOSPEL LIGHT

We've come this far by faith
Leaning on the Lord;
Trusting in His Holy Word,
He's never failed me yet.
Oh—can't turn around,
We've come this far by faith.

—Albert A. Goodson

In the moment of quiet as the voices of Jesse Semple's choir singing the old gospel hymn died away, Geneva appeared in the pulpit. At sight of her regal figure in the gold robe her Curia Sisters had bestowed on her, the congregation caught its collective breath, then settled back in awed expectation. The church, almost full when the service began, was now packed. Ushers had brought folding chairs from the big community room downstairs. Despite their efforts, dozens of worshipers stood in the back aisle. Evidently, interest in and questions about Geneva Crenshaw had moved church members to come out in droves.

"Your choir," she began, her voice resonating with a peculiar power through the high-ceilinged church, "is a blessing to you and an inspiration to me. When they sing, there is no doubt in my heart, no doubt whatsoever, that the Lord is in His Holy Temple. Choir music, especially the joyous music of gospel, imbues us with the exaltation that must have moved the Psalmist when he wrote for all the ages:

> I was glad when they said unto me,
> Let us go into the House of the Lord.

"And this Sunday morning, the Lord is here because that music cannot be denied. It is the music we have known all our lives. We knew the music before we knew our faith, and when we gained faith, this was the music of our faith. It is the music that throughout our lives accompanies our going out and our coming in, our waking up and our lying down. And when in that last hour, we breathe our last breath, the songs of Zion will be, if not on our lips, at least deep in our souls, and there they will remain forever. Thank God for the music. Amen."

"Amen, sister!" one man replied. "Praise the Lord," the deacons responded. There was a smattering of relieved applause. They had come to hear this woman about whom so much was said, but had not expected a serious sermon, one they could sink their souls into. Geneva was obviously going to give them exactly that.

"I don't know about you, but when I heard the choir raise that great hymn 'We've Come This Far by Faith,' heard them sing it in the gospel tradition, I found it difficult to imagine that these glorious sounds were once banned from churches like this one."

"Well." An old man spoke his one-word acknowledgment in the tradition.

"Given the age of this building, I would not be surprised to learn that your predecessors at one time banned the Negro spirituals, the music our enslaved ancestors left us as a legacy, to remind us of those who survived the world's most vicious servitude."

"Preach, sister, preach!"

"We can forgive them, Church. The early leaders of the black church wanted to show white people that black people were worthy of citizenship, and could worship in a dignified manner, without the emotional outcries that went back to the days when the slaves had to sneak off and hold 'bush meetings,' where they clapped and shouted, sang and danced. You understand! Slavery was defined by silent obedience. In religion, forced silence could give way to sound. 'Make a joyful noise unto the Lord' had a special meaning. Can I get a witness?"

"Yes, it did! Teach, Sister Geneva! Teach!"

"Black religion was born of need and sanctified in joyful noise. After Emancipation though, some black churches, seeking acceptance by white denominations, reined in their worship services to conform with the restrained rituals of white churches. Commitment to this emulation led some Northern black churches to believe that emotional worship was considered heathenish, redolent of Africa, just plain unwhite. In what they hoped would prove the Promised Land, God was worshiped à la Mozart. Sad, Church. Sad, but true. They learned the hard way that black choirs singing European music, even under the direction of highly trained directors, were still black and, therefore—for most of the white world—unacceptable.

"Later, when the spirituals gained a measure of acceptance in our churches, it was gospel music, the music of a free but still subordinated and despised people, that was deemed too secular, too much like jazz, the music of the clubs, the honky-tonks, the after-hours joints. You know that what I say is true. Can I get a witness?"

"It's true! It sure is true!" half the congregation responded. Others nodded their heads, waved their fans, smiled, and poked their neighbors in the ribs. "This sermon goin' to be a treat 'stead of a treatment," one sister said. Her neighbor nodded, "Hush, don't want to miss a word."

"Change did not come easy," Geneva reminded them. "It never does. It was slow. It had to overcome great resistance. As with everything worthwhile in this life, the acceptance of gospel music took courage, it took struggle, it took sacrifice. Somebody, probably the minister, had to decide. He had to get up in this pulpit and tell everybody that he decided, 'I'm not goin' to let the Devil have all the best tunes. Not goin' to do it. Music that good, Devil must have stole it. Church, we gwine to steal it back.' That must have been how gospel came to the black church. That preacher had to risk his popularity, his support, maybe even his job.

"You know it. I know it. We all know it. There are times when the Lord expects you to move away from comfort, move away from safety, move away from security, and reach out and take a sacrificial risk. You know what the traditional hymn tells us:

> *Jesus walked that lonesome valley, he had to walk it*
> *by himself, and*
> *You have to walk that lonesome valley, you have to*
> *walk it for yourself,*
> *For nobody else can walk it for you, you have to walk*
> *it for yourself.*

"Now hear me, Church! Walking that lonesome valley, taking that risk is not about the risk some people take in playing the lottery. And I am not talking a calculated risk in sports or in competing for a new job. Neither am I talking about a romantic risk, when you tell someone you care and, in the telling, risk rejection. Church, I am talking about a sacrificial risk, one that could cost you a lot, maybe everything, and you make it not for self, not even for a loved one, not for a friend, but a risk on

behalf of someone who has done you wrong and you have for-
given them for it. One you do for folks you don't even know.
One for a cause you know is right even when the whole world
thinks it is wrong. I hope the Church understands what I am
saying this morning."

Geneva paused. Her eyes swept across the congregation.
When they met mine, she smiled and nodded ever so briefly. "I
hope there is someone out there this morning who knows
about sacrificial risks and recognizes that, though there be loss,
out of that loss can come the gain of glory.

"This morning, I want to tell you one story about how one
church came to see the light, the Gospel Light."

With the start of her story, Geneva eased from the ringing
rhetoric of the black minister to the calm, even style of story-
telling I knew so well. The congregation quieted until there
was hardly a sound other than Geneva's rich contralto weaving
a portrait with words.

❧

She seldom heard her given name. Everyone, even her mother,
called her Melodie. She was in her middle twenties, quite tall,
skinny, and very dark. She was fairly ordinary in every way but
one. The woman could sing. Always could, and the older she
got, the better she sounded. She sang her first church solo at
age four and was moved up to the senior choir at ten, much to
the dismay of the children's choir director. Melodie could solo
and fill in on any parts that were weak. Her ear was keen, she
read music, and, when the choir pianist was not available, she
could fill in there, too.

Melodie, like so many of our singers—Aretha Franklin,
Dinah Washington, Sam Cooke, Mahalia Jackson, so many others—had been brought up in the church. Melodie lived for the
First Tabernacle Baptist Church and for singing. A good thing,
too. For, except for Melodie, the music was—well, the music
was not impressive.

You see, First Tabernacle was where the black people in that medium-size town went who were trying to move up in the world, and who had, during the service, already moved beyond shouting and other—for them—embarrassing emotional displays. The choir sang "anthems." Sang them straight out of hymn books and sheet music purchased—they proudly told anyone who seemed at all interested—from the same sources as the white churches across town. At First Tabernacle, the Biblical command "Make a joyful noise unto the Lord" seemed to call for "A Mighty Fortress Is Our God," rather than "Ride On, King Jesus" or "Glory, Glory, Hallelujah" or "This Little Light of Mine."

Fact is, they seldom sang spirituals—dismissed them as primitive slave songs. And they did not sing gospel. In those days, when the black poor came up North, gospel became a sacred counterpart of the city blues, and it was sung in the same improvisatory tradition with piano, guitar, even drums. Gospel was definitely not heard in middle-class black churches like First Tabernacle, where "movin' on up" the economic ladder was the secular ideal.

Melodie's father was minister of First Tabernacle. He was a staunch defender of the church's "moving up" credo. He worshiped his God, dedicated himself to his church, and never failed to express his appreciation to his wife who, like many minister's wives, performed all manner of functions for the church and the congregation. The joy of his life, though, was Melodie. While her service to the church was beyond measure, the Reverend Munday made sure she went to a good college. There, she heard gospel music for the first time and began singing in the style that seemed made for her big, beautiful voice. She did not tell her father about her gospel singing. And when she expressed her decision to enroll in divinity school, he supported her, though with the warning that she would have a hard time as a woman getting a "call" to a good church.

Melodie finished divinity school with fine grades and great potential, but churches did not ask her to compete when they needed a new pastor. She returned to First Tabernacle and there assisted her father with communions and christenings, reading the Scripture during the sermons and, of course, handling the choir's solos, but she did not get a chance to preach. Even when her father was away, the church elders invited other ministers for guest sermons. All of them were, of course, men.

And one of them, Shadrach, was a son of the church. Like Melodie, he had gone to divinity school and now was pastor to a small church in a nearby town. They had been friends as children, and their relationship now showed the promise of romance—a result much desired by both their parents and the church membership. Shadrach shared Melodie's father's and—to tell the truth—most of the congregation's views about spirituals in the church and about women in the pulpit.

Melodie loved her father and her church, and might have served as unofficial assistant pastor until she married Shadrach and took up similar duties at his church. Fact is, she deferred answering his proposals of marriage because—well, because she felt God had a different fate in store for her. Then, late one Saturday night while preparing his sermon for the next morning, Melodie's father suffered a stroke. A few hours later, he died.

Melodie, overcome with grief, sang two solos at her father's funeral. The first, one of his favorite hymns, "His Eye Is on the Sparrow," brought tears and comfort to the congregation. It was, they felt, Melodie at her finest.

> *I sing because I'm happy, I sing because I'm free,*
> *For His eye is on the sparrow, And I know He watches*
> *me.*

Her second selection, though, caused great upset. Melodie accompanied herself and, standing beside the piano, she introduced the hymn in a quiet voice.

"Some years ago, the Reverend Thomas A. Dorsey, often called the father of gospel music, received word, while away on a trip, of the tragic death of his wife and first baby in childbirth. Out of his despair, he sought strength from God by writing a song I have come to love. I sing it today in the hope that it will provide me, our family, and this church with the consolation we need in this sad time."

Then she sang "Precious Lord."

> *Precious Lord, Take my hand, Lead me on, Let me stand.*
> *I am tired, I am weak, I am worn.*

Today, we would say Melodie sang that familiar gospel hymn in the sacred style of Mahalia Jackson. She left no note untouched; she extended each one, modulated it, embellished it with emotion. Melodie sang all the verses, concluding with the final lines of the refrain:

> *Through the dark, through the light, lead me on, to the light.*
> *Precious Lord, take my hand, lead me on.*

Everyone now knows this hymn—the favorite of Dr. Martin Luther King, Jr. Who of us has not been down and, using the words of that hymn, called on the Lord for help and strength? It brings back sad times as valleys traversed, as mountains scaled. But when Melodie sang this gospel hymn at her father's funeral, the congregation heard it in disbelief. It was, they said later, a "blasphemy."

There was even more shock when Melodie told the church

elders that she wished to be considered for the pastorship. With more reluctance than enthusiasm, the selection committee accepted her application and listed her as one of those who would give a trial sermon. No woman's name had ever been placed on that list in First Tabernacle's long history. They acted out of respect for Melodie's father, but for many on the church's boards and in its membership, a woman's place was in the home, not in the pulpit.

Whether because he was the best, or only the best known, Shadrach's sermon was well received, and most of the church was certain that he would become the next pastor of First Tabernacle. Melodie was advised, not very subtly, that it was best she withdraw. Her refusal annoyed the committee and hurt Shadrach.

"I forgive you for singing the Devil's song in church. Why won't you marry me and we can be a team doing God's work together?"

"In seeking to succeed my father, Shadrach, I *am* doing God's work."

Shadrach did not respond. Melodie knew that if she persisted in what he saw as an unseemly competition, their relationship would end. Why must a church team mean always the man in the pulpit and the woman willing to do much of the church's work, raising the money, visiting the sick, singing in the choir, keeping the books—so much of the work that makes the church a church? Women are assumed to be able to do all these things, but not to be able to preach. Why must the church work like the marriage model in the home?

There was for Melodie, as for so many of us, the choice not of wrong and right. Melodie and most of us, thank God, are able to resist the temptation of doing what we know is wrong. It is infinitely more difficult to choose between the easy way and the right way. Easy and right seem to go together. Melodie could see her future in First Tabernacle. Shadrach, set in his

ways though he was, would be a good pastor, a good husband
and father. Her life there would not be onerous. And yet what
seemed easy-right did not seem God-right. Not if there was
ever going to be change in this and in so much of life that
squelches the spirit in the name of tradition. How can change
come unless those who care refuse to follow in the old foot-
steps, refuse to take the easy way? She worried. She prayed. In
the meantime, the church elders, unaware of her turmoil,
reluctantly set a date for Melodie to present a trial sermon.
When they told her, she thought, God has decided.

As the date approached, the controversy grew. Lifelong
friends avoided her. Those who didn't urged her to withdraw
and were offended when she did not heed their pleas. Women
were probably worse than men on the subject of a woman minister, though, Lord knows, the men were bad enough. Trying to
bear the attacks on her with Christian tolerance, Melodie
thought often of the traditional spiritual "Scandalize' My Name."

> *Well, I met my sister de other day,*
> *give her my right hand,*
> *Jes' as soon as ever my back was turned*
> *She took 'n' scan-da-lize' my name.*
> *Do you call dat a sister?*
> *No! No! scan-da-lize' my name.*

Believing that God had inspired her decision to go forward
with her application, Melodie prayed for inspiration about what
to say in her sermon. But her efforts to prepare were fruitless.
What, she thought, can you say to people whose minds are
closed? The answer was clear: nothing. And that, she realized,
was the answer.

When she walked to the pulpit, she carried not a Bible, but
a book of hymns—not the one used at First Tabernacle, but
one put together by a relatively new church across town which

served black people recently arrived from the South. She stood in the pulpit for a long moment. When she finally spoke, her tone was calm, devoid of emotion.

"I forgive all those of you who called me evil names because I, a woman, seek to preach the word of God. This is my church, and I will always love it and you, its congregation. But this morning I am here not to please you, but rather to praise God in the fashion of His gifts to me." Then, without further introduction or accompaniment, she began to sing gospel hymns from the book: "How I Got Over," "Just to Behold His Face," "Surely, God Is Able." She closed with "We've Come This Far by Faith." It was, as some witnesses conceded later, a sermon in concert, which should have opened all but blinded eyes and sealed hearts—as, sadly, were those of that congregation.

At the close of her last hymn, Melodie stood in the pulpit, looking out at all those still, closed faces looking back at her. Everyone was stunned by the beauty of her music, but determined—despite some inner turbulence—not to be moved by it.

Melodie did not offer a closing prayer. As benediction, she raised her hands in blessing over the congregation and sang the prayer they all knew:

> *If I have wounded any souls today,*
> *If I have caused one foot to go astray,*
> *If I have walked in my own willful way,*
> *Dear Lord, Forgive.*

After several minutes, as the congregation still sat silent, Melodie raised the hymnal above her head. Its cover caught and reflected a shaft of light from the great rose window high above the pulpit. They all saw the light. They were all afraid. Only in soft whispers did they acknowledge later that it was not a reflection. Truly, it was a gospel light.

Melodie left the pulpit and walked slowly down the center aisle and out the great front doors of the church. She had rejected the predictable, the prudent, the easy way. Ahead lay scary challenge along risk-filled, pathless ways. Melodie did not know where trying to do God's work would take her. She knew only that her way would be guided by the gospel light.

Shadrach served the First Tabernacle Baptist Church for many years with distinction. At some point much later in the church's history, its records note a number of the congregation's favorite hymns. All of them were gospel songs.

∞

"Let the church say, Amen," said Geneva at her story's end.

"Amen!" they responded.

Then she motioned toward Semple in the choir. He stood and sang one chorus of "We've Come This Far by Faith." He sang quietly, reverently. Then, the choir stood and joined him, picking up the tempo, adding modulations and rhythm. Semple motioned to the congregation, who needed little encouragement to stand and join in. No longer a simple hymn of reverence, it was now a great jubilee, ending in a cascade of sound that touched and moved the heart in each one of us there that day.

My wife grasped my arm. "Look!" she said. "Geneva's gone!"

"Yes." I had already noticed her slipping away when the choir stood to sing. "She has given her all for all of us. It is up to us now to do what we can for one another."

~

ACKNOWLEDGMENTS

As every author knows, and most are willing to acknowledge, a good editor is an essential monitor of creative excess, a passionate exterminator of grammatical error. Phoebe Hoss, editor of each of my books published by Basic Books, once again brought order to my ideas and comprehension to my writing. Lynn Walker Huntley, formerly of the Ford Foundation, facilitated my research with a grant supporting this and other writing projects. My agent, Faith Hampton Childs, in addition to her representational functions, also read drafts and offered reassurance at critical times. New York University Law School Dean John Sexton has continued to provide a base for my teaching and research funds; and the MacDowell Colony provided a creative environment in which I wrote an early draft. Janet Dewart Bell brought to her review of several drafts her skills as an editor and her love as my wife. My sons, Derrick, Douglass, and Carter Bell, assured me that my writing was in tune with aspects of contemporary life. Linda Singer, Odetta MacLeish, and Amy Redling helped with the research. A host of friends and students gave me sound advice and insights about the perils and priceless experience of womanhood in this society. They include: Lisa Boykin, Judy Randall, Tanya Coke,

Gwen Jordan, Jane Manning, Elaine Grant, Suzette Malveaux, Sherry Lee, Deborah Creane, Gayle Wintjen, Claudia Rankine, Sarah Schulman, Linda Villarosa, Robert Verhaaren, and Paulette J. Robinson. Lawrence Watson, and Phyllis Locus of the Rainbow Music Company in Harlem helped me find my way through the rich field of gospel music. Alan Levine helped with some arcane legal issues. Jennifer Haus handled secretarial chores. Finally, I wish to acknowledge two former Basic Books officials, who supported my writing: the late Martin Kessler, until recently president and editorial director at Basic Books, who first provided a publishing home for my nontraditional writing; and the late Lois Shapiro, former vice president and marketing director whose efforts on my behalf led to real friendship.

NOTES

Epigraph

Page

vii James Weldon Johnson, "O Black and Unknown Bards," *St. Peter Relates an Incident* (New York: Viking Penguin, 1993), p. 25.

Prologue

Page

1 *"We're not here for no form . . . "*: A traditional greeting used by gospel groups.

1 *"make a joyful noise unto the Lord"*: Psalm 94,4.

2 The insight about "good news" and "gospel truth" is from Paul Oliver, Max Harrison, and William Bolcom, *Gospel, Blues and Jazz* (New York: Norton, 1980), p. 199.

2 "you have to be able . . . ": Bernice Johnson Reagon, "Singing for My Life," in Bernice Johnson Reagon, ed., *We Who Believe in Freedom* (New York: Anchor Books/Doubleday, 1993), pp. 133, 141.

3 "an enhanced mode of communication . . . ": Paul Gilroy, *The Black Atlantic: Modernity and Double Consciousness* (Cambridge, Mass.: Harvard University Press, 1993), p. 76.

3 "inoculation against poison . . . ": Alice Walker, "Introduction: Sweet Honey in the Rock—The Sound of Our Own Culture," in Reagon, *We Who Believe*, p. 9.

3 "the journal of a lifetime . . . ": Susan L. Taylor, *Lessons in Living* (New York: Anchor Books, Doubleday, 1995), p. 13.

4 The Dallas/Fort Worth Mass Choir can be heard singing "Look How Far We've Come" on *Glory Train* (Malaco Records, Inc., MCD 2012, Jackson, Miss.), disc 1.

5 The white men responding to the Million Man March were both quoted in Sam Howe Verhover, "Million Man March Puzzles a Houston Suburb," *New York Times,* Oct. 19, 1995, p. A16.

6 Robert Reich's figures and statement were found in Karen De Witt, "Black Men Say the March in Washington Is About Them, Not Farrakhan," *New York Times*, Oct. 15, 1995, p. 22.

7 The ratios of earnings are from Jeremy Rifkin, *The End of Work: The Decline of the Global Labor Force and the Dawn of the Post-Market Era* (New York: Putnam, 1995), p. 173.

7 "Americans are right to be worried . . . ": Michael Mandel, "The Real Truth About the Economy," *Business Week* (Nov. 7, 1994) p. 110.

7 ". . . no one dreams of saying": John Kenneth Galbraith, "Recession? Why Worry?," *New York Times*, May 12, 1993, p. A 19.

8 an international study on income distribution: "Widest Gap in Incomes? Research Points to U.S.," *New York Times,* Oct. 27, 1995, p. D 2.

8 income inequalities in America: "Inequality: For Richer, for Poorer," *The Economist*, Nov. 5, 1994, p. 19.

9 Edward Luttwack's warning and his examples come from his article "Will Success Spoil America: Why the Pols Don't Get Our Real Crisis of Values," *Washington Post*, Nov. 27, 1994, p. C 1.

10 As a guest on this "Donahue," which was broadcast on February 8, 1993, I witnessed this incident.

12 my 1987 book: Derrick Bell, *And We Are Not Saved: The Elusive Quest for Racial Justice* (New York: Basic Books, 1987).

12 my second book: Derrick Bell, *Faces at the Bottom of the Well: The Permanence of Racism* (New York: Basic Books, 1992).

13 "'I tremble for my country . . .'": Jefferson is quoted in Donald Robinson, *Slavery in the Structure of American Politics: 1760–1820* (New York: Harcourt Brace, Jovanovich, 1971), p. 92.

15 "'do not come from people . . .'": Walker, in Reagon, *We Who Believe*, p. 9.

16 Marion Williams, "I'm Going to Live the Life I Sing About in My Song," on *Precious Lord: Recordings of the Great Gospel Songs of Thomas A. Dorsey* (Columbia/Legacy CK 57164).

Chapter 1. Redemption Deferred: Back to the Space Traders

Page

18 The summary of "The Space Traders" is from Derrick Bell, *Faces at the Bottom of the Well*, pp. 158–94. The quotation is on p. 158.

24 Geneva's gospel hymn is "'blacks would just go away . . .'": Patricia J. Williams, "The Executioner's Automat," *The Nation* 261 (July 10, 1995), pp. 59, 63.

24 "'[l]ift every voice and sing': The anthem is "Soon-a Will Be Done," Traditional, in *Songs of Zion* (Nashville, Tenn.: Abingdon Press, 1981), p. 158.

27 the André Crouch gospel song: André Crouch, "Soon and Very Soon," *Songs of Zion*, p. 198.

27 "[s]omething you somehow haven't to deserve": Robert Frost, "The Death of the Hired Man," *Collected Poems of Robert Frost* (New York: Garden City Publishing, 1942), p. 53.

28 John Newton, "Amazing Grace," in *Songs of Zion*, p. 211.

Chapter 2. Trying to Teach the White Folks

Page

29 "I have never reached perfection . . .": Thomas A. Dorsey, "Lord I've Tried," quoted in Wyatt Tee Walker, *Somebody's Calling My Name: Black Sacred Music and Social Change* (Valley Forge, Pa.: Judson Press, 1979), p. 150.

30 "'will never gain full equality . . .'": Derrick Bell, *Faces at the Bottom of the Well*, p. 12.

36 "the journalist Ellis Cose": Ellis Cose, *The Rage of a Privileged Class* (New York: HarperCollins, 1993). See also Joe R. Feagin and Melvin P. Sikes, *Living with Racism: The Black Middle-Class Experience* (Boston: Beacon Press, 1994).

37 "'treat the genuine pathologies . . .'": Michael Lind, "To Have and Have Not: Notes on the Progress of the American Class War," *Harper's* (June 1995), pp. 35, 38. Lind's views are expressed at length in his *The Next American Nation* (New York: Free Press, 1994); see also Charles A. Reich, *Opposing the System* (New York: Crown, 1995).

38 "an article that suggests we have a federal law": Derrick Bell, "The Freedom of Employment Act," *The Nation* (May 23, 1994), p. 708.

43 "'already well into a shift . . .'": Jeremy Rifkin, *The End of Work* (New York: Putnam, 1994).

45 "a third-world economy": Bernard Sanders, "Whither American Democracy?" *Los Angeles Times,* Jan. 16, 1994, p. M-5; Noam Chomsky, *Year 501: The Conquest Continues* (Boston: South End Press, 1993).

Chapter 3. Living with the Specter of Calhoun

Page

49 Evening Prayer, Traditional. The hymn is beautifully sung by Mahalia Jackson on *Newport, 1958, Mahalia Jackson,* (Columbia, CS 8071).

51 "From its inception as a radio serial . . .": Bart Andrews and Ahrgus Juilliard, *Holy Mackerel!: The Amos 'n' Andy Story* (New York: Dutton, 1986), p. xix.

51 "an extraordinary type . . . an economic adversary": Joseph Boskin, *Sambo: The Rise and Demise of an American Jester* (New York: Oxford University Press, 1986), pp. 13–14.

52 "Either I can play a maid . . .": McDaniel is quoted in ibid., p. 83.

52 the constant pressure of the NAACP: Melvin Ely, *The Adventures of Amos 'n' Andy* (New York: Free Press, 1991).

54 "in the popular imagination . . .": Ishmael Reed, "Crime,

Drugs and the Media: The Black Pathology Biz," in Peter Rothberg, ed., *Uncivil War: Race, Civil Rights and "The Nation": 1865–1995* (New York: The Nation Press, 1995), p. 27.

55 "new, black, public intellectuals": See, for example, Michael Berube, "Public Academy," *The New Yorker* 73 (Jan. 9, 1995); Robert Boynton, "The New Intellectuals," *Atlantic Monthly* 53 (Mar. 1995); Hortense Spillers, "The Crisis of the Negro Intellectual: A Post-Date," *Boundary* 2 (Fall 1994), p. 65.

56 "Black intellectual life . . . ": Cornel West, "The Dilemma of the Black Intellectual" in bell hooks and Cornell West, *Breaking Bread* (Boston: South End Press, 1991), pp. 131, 137.

56 "As with Washington . . . ": Adolph Reed, "What Are the Drums Saying, Booker?" *The Village Voice* 40 (Apr. 11, 1995), pp. 31, 34.

57 "acting just like a nigger" . . . "only those who have tried . . . ": James Baldwin, "East River, Downtown," in James Baldwin, *The Price of the Ticket: Collected Nonfiction 1948–1985* (New York: Marek/St. Martin's, 1985), pp. 263, 268.

57 "to take to the rostrum . . . ": Harold Cruse, *The Crisis of the Negro Intellectual* (New York: Morrow, 1967), pp. 455–56.

Chapter 4. Staying "No Ways Tired"

Page

60 *"I don't feel no ways tired . . . "*: The epigraph (repeated at chapter's end) is from James Cleveland, "I Don't Feel No Ways Tired," on *Rev. James Cleveland: A Tribute to the King* (Malaco Records, MAL 2009 CD), disc 1.

65 *The Bell Curve:* Richard J. Herrnstein and Charles Murray, *The Bell Curve: Intelligence and Class Structure in American Life* (New York: Free Press, 1994).

67 "rational discrimination": Dinesh D'Souza, *The End of Racism* (New York: Free Press, 1995), pp. 245–87.

67 For a selection of the responses to *The Bell Curve,* see Steven Fraser, ed., *The Bell Curve Wars* (New York: Basic Books, 1995).

69 For the lynching outside Memphis and its ramifications, see Paula Giddings, *When and Where I Enter: The Impact of Black Women on Race and Sex in America* (New York: Morrow, 1984), pp. 17–18.

69 historians such as Eric Foner: Foner's discussion of retaliation against blacks is in his *Reconstruction: America's Unfinished Revolution 1863–1877* (New York: Harper & Row, 1988), pp. 425–44. The farmer is quoted on p. 429.

Chapter 5. The Freedom of Employment Act

Page

74 *"If the world from you withhold . . . ":* Charles A. Tindley, "Leave It There," *Songs of Zion,* p. 23.

74 Derrick Bell, "The Freedom of Employment Act," *The Nation* (May 23, 1994), p. 708.

78 *Brown* v. *Board of Education:* 347 U.S. 483 (1954).

79 "saleable commodity" . . . "voluntary abortions": Jonathan Swift, *The Portable Swift,* edited by Carl Van Doren (New York: Penguin, 1948, 1976), pp. 550, 551.

Chapter 6. Shadow Song

Page

91 *"I'm com'in' up . . . ":* Rev. F. C. Barnes, *Rough Side of the Mountain* on "Live" (Atlanta International Record Co., AIR10209, 1995).

95 "as though we are the threat": On the situation of black lesbians, see generally Catherine E. McKinley and Joyce DeLaney, eds., *Afrekete: An Anthology of Black Lesbian Writing* (New York: Anchor Books/Doubleday, 1995).

95–96 an article in *Essence* magazine: Linda Villarosa, "Revelations," *Essence* (Sept. 1995), p. 90. See also Linda Villarosa, "Coming Out," *Essence* (May 1991), p. 82.

96 the first chapter of Romans: Holy Bible, Revised Standard

Version (1953), which is also the source for the 1 Timothy quotation.

96 "Audre Lorde, Dionne Brand, Sarah Schulman": For these writers on lesbian discrimination, see Audre Lorde, *Sister Outsider* (Freedom, Calif.: Crossing Press, 1984); Dionne Brand, *Bread Out of Stone* (Morton Grove, Ill.: Coach House Press, 1994); and Sarah Schulman, *My American History: Lesbian and Gay Life Through the Reagan-Bush Years* (New York: Routledge, 1994).

96 "The Supreme Court": I am referring to the Court's decision in *Bowers* v. *Hardwick,* 478 U.S. 186 (1986), in which by a 5–4 decision the Court refused to find a right of privacy protection from prosecution under Georgia's sodomy statute, homosexual acts performed in a private home.

100 "Crispus Attucks": John Hope Franklin and Alfred A. Moss Jr., *From Slavery to Freedom,* 6th ed. (New York: Alfred A. Knopf, 1988), pp. 65–66.

101 " '[f]aith without works is dead' ": Holy Bible, King James Version, James 2:20.

101 " 'love is not love . . . ' ": Sonnet 116, G. Blakemore Evans, ed., *Riverside Shakespeare* (Boston: Houghton Mifflin, 1974), p. 1770.

102 " 'Over time I came to realize . . . ' ": Audre Lorde, *Zami: A New Spelling of My Name* (Watertown, Mass.: Persephone Press, 1982), p. 204.

Chapter 7. The Mentality of Race

Page

103 "*Courage my soul . . .* ": Charles A. Tindley, "The Storm Is Passing Over," in *Songs of Zion,* p. 58.

Chapter 8. Nigger Free

Page

115 "*We have come over a way . . .* ": James Weldon Johnson and J. Rosamond Johnson, "Lift Every Voice and Sing," *Songs of Zion,* p. 32.

115–16 "a coordinated plan . . . ": Tony Barta, "Relations of Genocide: Land and Lives in the Colonization of Australia," in
Isidor Walliman and Michael Dobkowski, eds., *Genocide
and the Modern Age* (Westport, Conn.: Greenwood Press,
1987), pp. 237–38.

116–17 "I could not but feel . . . ": James Baldwin, *The Fire Next
Time* (New York: The Dial Press, 1963), p. 67.

117 The details about the Mormons are from The Church of
Jesus Christ of Latter-Day Saints, *Church History in the
Fullness of Times* (Salt Lake City: The Church of Jesus
Christ of Latter-Day Saints, 1989); the quotations are from
The Church of Jesus Christ of Latter-Day Saints, *History
of the Church*, 4:80.

118 The Philadelphia riot is reported in Peter Bergman, *The
Chronological History of the Negro in America* (New York:
Harper & Row, 1969), pp. 149–50.

118 Throughout the antebellum years . . . :David Roediger, *The
Wages of Whiteness* (New York: Verso, 1991), pp. 100–10.

118–19 Events in the New York City riot reported in Iver Bern-
stein, *The New York City Draft Riots* (New York: Oxford
University Press, 1990), pp. 6–9, 27–31, 48.

119–20 "A child of 3 years of age . . . ": Eric Foner, *Reconstruction:
America's Unfinished Revolution 1863–1877* (New York:
Harper & Row, 1988), p. 33.

120 forty-six blacks and two whites: Bergman, *Chronological
History*, p. 252.

120 "inconceivably brutal . . . ": E. L. Godkin, "The Moral of
the Memphis Riots," in Peter Rothberg, ed., *Uncivil War:
Race, Civil Rights and "The Nation": 1865–1995* (New
York: The Nation Press, 1995), p. 3.

120–21 The Colfax riot is reported in Foner, *Reconstruction*, p. 437.

121 Four years later, the Supreme Court: *United States* v.
Cruikshank, 92 U.S. 542 (1876).

121 Details about the Atlanta riot are from John Hope Franklin
and Alfred A. Moss Jr., *From Slavery to Freedom*, 6th ed.
(New York: Alfred A. Knopf, 1988), p. 283.

121 The East St. Louis riot is reported by Elliott Rudwick,
"Race Riot at East St. Louis, July 2, 1917," in Anthony

Platt, ed., *The Politics of Riot Commissions* (New York: Collier, 1971), p. 83.

122 Wilson, like most of America's presidents: Kenneth O'Reilly, *Nixon's Piano: Presidents and Racial Politics from Washington to Clinton* (New York: Free Press, 1995), pp. 91–92.

122 "...he lay helpless in the street": Platt, *Politics of Riot Commissions*, p. 64.

122–23 "All fared alike ...": "Report on the Special Committee Authorized by Congress to Investigate the East St. Louis Riots" in ibid., pp. 59, 63–64.

123 "The police shot ...": Ibid., pp. 69–80.

123 "Red Summer": Johnson, quoted in Franklin and Moss, *From Slavery to Freedom*, p. 313.

124 Policemen who came on the scene ...: Ibid., p. 98.

124 Total casualties of Chicago riot are from Chicago Commission on Race Relations, "The Negro in Chicago: A Study of Race Relations and a Race Riot," in Platt, ed., *Politics of Riot Commissions*, pp. 97–101.

124–25 The Elaine, Arkansas, riot is reported in Lee Williams and Lee Williams Jr., *Anatomy of Four Race Riots* (Jackson, Miss.: University and College Press of Mississippi, 1992), pp. 38–55.

126 "The heaviest fighting ...": Ibid., p. 56.

127 "People came from all around": Lori Rozsa, "Massacre in a Small Town in 1923," *Atlanta Journal and Constitution*, Jan. 17, 1993, p. M 1. See also William Booth, "Rosewood," *Washington Post*, May 30, 1993, p. F1.

128 a controversial claim bill ...: "Comments: House Bill 591: Florida Compensates Rosewood Victims and Their Families for a Seventy-One-Year-Old Injury," *Florida State University Law Review* 22 (1994), p. 503.

128 years between 1859 and 1969: Ralph Ginzburg, *One Hundred Years of Lynchings* (Baltimore: Black Classic Press 1969, 1988 ed.).

128 "little to fear from those ...": M. Belknap, *Federal Law and Southern Order* (Athens: University of Georgia Press, 1995), pp. 8–9.

128–29 G. H. White: Peter M. Bergman, *Chronological History,* p. 330.

129 "North America does not need . . .": Dionne Brand, *Bread out of Stone* (Morton Grove, Ill.: Coach House Press, 1994), pp. 116–17.

130 conclusion in the 1930s: James Weldon Johnson, *Negro Americans: What Now?* (New York: Viking Press, 1934).

Chapter 9. Racial Royalties

Page

141 *"Throw out the life line . . . ":* Edward S. Ufford, in *Songs of Zion,* p. 56.

145 *"Tempted and tried . . . ":* "Farther Along," *Songs of Zion,* p. 28.

146–47 *"You've taken my blues . . . ":* Langston Hughes's poem appears in his "Note on Commercial Theatre," in Arnold Rampersad, ed., Vol. I, *The Life of Langston Hughes, 1902–1941* (New York: Oxford University Press, 1986), p. 381.

Chapter 10. Women to the Rescue

Page

152 *"Speak to my heart . . . ":* New York Restoration Choir, "Speak to My Heart," on *Glory Train* (Malaco Music, Inc., MCD 2012), disc 2.

156 "what black women have done . . .": Jacqueline Jones, *Labor of Love, Labor of Sorrow* (New York: Vintage, 1986).

157 " 'the action of the White Republic . . . ' ": James Baldwin, *The Evidence of Things Not Seen* (New York: Henry Holt, 1985, 1995), p. 21.

158 " 'universal mystery of men' ": Ibid., p. 20.

159 " 'a man cannot bear . . . a train and rides' ": Ibid., pp. 20–21.

160 " 'life ain't been no crystal stair' ": Joy James and Ruth Farmer, eds., *Spirit, Space and Survival: African American Women in (White) Academe* (New York: Routledge, 1993).

162 "Rounding a corner . . .": Amitav Ghosh, "The Ghosts of Mrs. Gandhi," *The New Yorker* (July 17, 1995), p. 40

Chapter 11. The Electric Slide Protest

Page

164 *"When I think . . . "*: "I Am a Soldier," A Celebration Song, Traditional, recorded by Vickie Winans on *Let's Get It On, a Sermon by Iona Locke* (Intersound Records, PDK 9128).

170–71 lyrics by Marcia Griffiths: Marcia Griffiths, "Electric Boogie on Carousel" (Island Records, 422–842 334–2).

171 *"I'm so glad, trouble . . . "*: Timothy Wright, "Trouble Don't Last Always," on *Glory Train* (Malaco Music, Inc., MCD 2012, Jackson, Miss.), disc 1.

Chapter 12. Equality's Child

Page

174 *"There is no pain . . . "*: Yolanda Adams, "The Battle Is the Lord's," on *Black Gospel Explosion II* (Nashville, Tenn.: New Haven Records, 8441875442).

177 public television series: "Equality." The filmmaker was Lourdes Portillo; the producer was Renee Tajima.

185 Professor Patricia Williams: Patricia Williams, "Alchemical Notes: Reconstructing Ideals from Deconstructed Rights," in J. Lobel, ed., *A Less Than Perfect Union: Alternative Perspectives on the United States Constitution* (New York: Monthly Review Press, 1988), p. 56.

Chapter 13. The Entitlement

Page

188 *"There are some things . . . "*: Kenneth Morris, "Yes, God Is Real," *Songs of Zion*, p. 201.

189 "mate swapping, men who beat women . . . ": Jill Nelson, "Talk Is Cheap," *The Nation* (June 5, 1995), p. 800.

Chapter 14. The Gospel Light

Page

203 *"We've come this far ... "*: Albert A. Goodson, "We've Come This Far by Faith," *Songs of Zion*, p. 192.

204 *"I was glad when ... "*: Psalm 122:1.

206 *"Jesus walked that ... "*: This traditional hymn, "Jesus Walked That Lonesome Valley," appears in many collections.

208 gospel became a sacred counterpart ... : Eileen Southern, *The Music of Black Americans* (New York: Norton, 1971); and Wyatt Tee Walker, *Somebody's Calling My Name* (Valley Forge, Pa.: Judson Press, 1979).

209 *"I sing because I'm happy ... "*: Harmonizing Four, "His Eyes Is on the Sparrow," on 22 *Original Gospel Greats* (Hollywood HCD-420).

210 *"Precious Lord, Take my hand ... "*: "Precious Lord," on *Precious Lord: Recordings of the Great Gospel Songs of Thomas A. Dorsey* (Columbia/Legacy CK 57164).

212 *"Well, I met my sister ... "*: "Scandalize My Name," *Songs of Zion*, p. 159.

213 *"If I have wounded ... "*: Evening Prayer. This traditional hymn is found in many places.